PROBATE

*A Practical Guide
For Settling an Estate*

©1981, 1986 HALT, Inc.

Primary Author: Mathew Valencic
Coauthor: Michael Richards
Editors: Paul Hasse, Michael Kress and Richard Hébert
Special Research and Writing: Barbara Alford, Jenefer Ellingston, Daniel Lewolt, Thomas Mostowy, Barry Stern and L. Margarette Williams
Third Edition Research: Bart Church, Michele Finger and Kay Ostberg
Graphics and Production: Bob Schmitt

Our thanks to the following attorneys, accountants and consumer specialists for their invaluable comments and advice: Dale E. Adams, Thomas Callahan, Richard J. Cardali, Sr., Carol Contrada, Gordon C. Gobel, Robert Dale Heron, Sophie Heymann, David L. Scull and John M. Sensenig.

First Edition: 1981
Second Edition: 1983
Third Edition: December, 1986
ISBN 0-910073-02-3

Also by HALT:

> Using a Lawyer
> Using a Law Library
> Small Claims Court
> Estate Planning
> Divorce
> Courts & Judges
> Real Estate

CONTENTS

1	Introduction
5	At a Glance
11	The Will
19	The Personal Representative
23	Estate Administration
27	Estate Inventory
33	Creditors' Claims
37	Real Estate Sales
39	Property Transfers
49	Taxes
55	Probate Fees
63	Closing the Estate
67	Distributing the Assets
71	Small-Estate Administration
77	Conclusion
79	P. R. Checklist
83	Appendix I: State Rules
139	Appendix II: Taxes

©1981, 1986 HALT, Inc.
An Organization of Americans for Legal Reform

INTRODUCTION

What is probate? Literally, the word *probate* means *prove*. Legally, it refers to the act of *proving a will*. It is the legal process of establishing the validity of the last will and testament of a deceased person (referred to in the law as the *decedent*). Popularly, the word *probate* has become synonymous with the entire body of law and procedures for estate administration — including proof of the will's validity, inventory and appraisal of the estate, payment of state and federal taxes and the administration and distribution of the estate's assets.

This manual is written primarily for the *personal representative* of an estate. The personal representative is the person named in the will or appointed by the court to administer an estate. Because the burden of responsibility for estate administration falls on the personal representative, the personal representative is the one who most needs practical advice about the probate process. But this manual also includes all the information needed by anyone else interested in following or participating in the probate of an estate.

If you are faced with acting as a personal representative for an estate and have not had any experience, you may have been led to believe that the probate system is too complicated and intimidating to enter on your own -- particularly if you are feeling the emotional stress that usually accompanies the death of a loved one. In fact, the administration of an estate is most often one of the simplest and most routine procedures in the American legal system. If you can make lists, add and subtract and ask questions, you can probably handle probate with ease.

A Word About Terms

It is almost impossible to discuss probate without using legal terms foreign to everyday language. In many cases, common words could replace the legal terms with no loss of meaning (for example, *deceased* instead of *decedent*). At other times, terms with particular legal meanings are used by the professionals interchangeably with more common terms (e.g., *devisees* or *beneficiaries* with *heirs*.)

This manual attempts to balance the use of common terms (such as *heirs*) with the terms that will arise time and again during the course of estate administration (such as *beneficiaries*).

When legal terms are used in this manual, they are followed by a definition or explanation. This will help you become familiar with the words and phrases you will find on forms and hear from lawyers, the probate registrar and tax authorities. If you become familiar with the basic vocabulary of probate, you should be able to handle the administration of an estate with greater confidence and efficiency.

How To Use This Manual

Before attempting to probate an estate on your own or turning it over to a lawyer, *you should read this manual all the way through at least once.* Such a first reading will give you an overview of the major issues and procedures involved and help you determine how you should administer the estate, when you should hire professional help, what additional information you need and where you can get it.

Once you begin the probate process, you should return to the manual a second time and concentrate on the sections or appendices that apply specifically to the estate you are administering.

A handy checklist of the basic steps a personal representative must perform begins at the end of the concluding chapter. Use it to remind yourself of the tasks you must complete before closing the estate. Also, the appendices at the back include information about probate statutes and tax schedules for all 50 states and the U.S. government.

At times, the information in this manual will have to be supplemented by additional reading or inquiries. The publications distributed by state and federal tax authorities are useful for completing tax returns, and personnel at the probate court in many jurisdictions can be excellent sources of help.

Dealing With the Probate Code

This manual includes in Appendix I all the current state-specific information you need to probate most estates. This information comes for the most part from your state's *probate code*, that part of your state's statutes that contains your state's probate laws.

If you have any questions about this information or wish to make sure it is current, you can check your probate code. You will need to locate the nearest public law library. (These are listed in HALT's manual, **Using a Law Library**.) The law librarian will tell you where to find your state code.

Appendix I of this manual includes code section numbers. Use these numbers to find the sections you want. Alternatively, you can use the index of the code. Be sure to check the latest updates of the code. These are contained in the pocket section at the end of each volume. A law dictionary for the layperson will be helpful if you have trouble understanding the code language.

Dealing With Court Personnel

Throughout this manual you will be referred to the *probate registrar* of the local court for specific information about local procedures. In some states or counties, the probate registrar may be called the *registrar of wills*, the *register of wills*, the *probate clerk* or simply the *clerk of the court*. These terms are used interchangeably in this manual. The probate registrar's assistants are also called clerks and can provide much of the basic information you will need.

The probate court staff are public employees who usually can provide the help you need. This does not mean you can expect them to probate the estate for you. Indeed, some probate court personnel, intimidated by lawyers and the threat of prosecution for "unauthorized practice of law," refuse to provide anything more than the most basic information. Others are simply impatient when dealing with the public and may refuse to take the time to help you.

The best approach is to tell them in a friendly way that you intend to go through the probate process on your own. Tell them you plan to learn how the process works and that you want the personal satisfaction of handling your own legal affairs. Explain that you would like to be able to ask their help at times, but that you will consult a lawyer for specific legal advice if it becomes necessary.

The clerks of the court will appreciate your recognition that they are limited in their ability to help you. A patient and courteous manner, combined with a desire to handle your own affairs, is more likely to obtain the help you need than an angry argument about your "rights."

Dealing With Lawyers

In many places, lawyers who do probate work charge not for the work they do but a percentage of the value of the estate being probated. You can save thousands of dollars by handling probate yourself or, if necessary, hiring a lawyer or accountant for an *hourly* fee to give you technical help on specific matters. Besides saving money, handling probate will enable you to enjoy the personal rewards of fulfilling family responsibilities or personal obligations through your own efforts.

Many competent lawyers, dissatisfied with the needless complexity and expense of probate, are willing to help you at reasonable hourly rates. Try to find one of these, using as a guide HALT's manual, **Using a Lawyer.**

Always remember, however, that it is not necessary to hire a lawyer to handle everything pertaining to probate. In most cases, probate does not include legal research and writing, adversary proceedings or other tasks requiring a lawyer's skills. For more information on hiring a lawyer and fees, see Chapter 10.

Chapter 1
AT A GLANCE

Everything outlined in this chapter will be discussed in detail in the step-by-step instructions that make up the remainder of this manual. This chapter simply gives an overview of the process so you can understand how the various parts fit together.

(1) Open the Estate for Probate

If the *decedent* (the deceased person) left a will, the original copy must be submitted to the probate court in the county where he or she resided. The will usually identifies the *personal representative* (P.R.) or *executor*. This person is responsible for administering the estate during the probate process.

If no valid will can be found, a personal representative must be appointed by the court, in which case the term *administrator* is often used. Someone who dies without writing a will is said to have died *intestate* and the assets of the estate must be distributed according to state law.

The personal representative must complete and file the proper forms with the probate court in order to *open* the estate. "Opening the estate" simply means beginning the probate process by notifying the court and all *interested persons* (relatives, heirs and creditors) of the death. A notice giving the names of all who have applied to be personal representative may also be required.

At this stage the personal representative may be able to choose from among several probate procedures (*supervised, unsupervised* or *small estate*), depending on the state in which the decedent lived and on the size and nature of the estate. These procedures are described in Chapters 4 and 13.

Once officially appointed, the personal representative will receive *letters of administration* (also called *letters testamentary*) from the probate registrar. These letters are the official evidence that the personal representative has the authority to act on behalf of the estate during the period of administration.

(2) Inventory the Estate

A rough estimate of the value of the *probate estate* may be required by the probate registrar at the time of application to open the estate. The probate estate consists of the decedent's personal and real property (real estate and buildings). However, most jointly-owned property, insurance benefits, pension plans and trusts are not included in the probate estate.

A detailed inventory and valuation of the probate estate must be filed with the court within one to six months from the opening of the estate, depending on the state. Several states require that this inventory include the entire estate (called the *gross estate*, which includes all the assets of the estate regardless of the form of ownership).

Estimates of the value of each item of property can easily be computed. Certain items, such as stocks and bonds, can be valued by checking the newspaper listings for the day of the death. Bank account balances can be obtained from the bank in which the accounts are held. Real estate and some items of valuable personal property may have to be appraised by court-appointed or privately hired appraisers. All of the necessary information and forms can be obtained from the probate registrar's office.

(3) Pay State and Federal Taxes

The *federal estate tax* is a steep, graduated tax, but as of 1986, it applies only if the value of *all* assets owned or partly-owned by the deceased exceeds $500,000. This amount increases to $600,000 for 1987 and years after, by which time it is estimated that fewer than one-third of one percent of all estates will need to file a federal estate tax return. (See Chapter 9 for further tax information.)

Every state except Nevada has some form of state death tax. A few have an *estate tax* much like the federal tax. The amount taxed varies from state to state, as do the rules governing how the rates apply. Other states impose a *credit estate tax* on estates that pay federal estate tax. This tax does not increase the amount of taxes owed because, in effect, it "rebates" part of the federal estate tax owed back to the state.

In many states, a beneficiary who inherits property has to pay an *inheritance tax* on the value of that property. The amount of the tax varies from state to state and depends on the size of the share and the relation of the heir to the decedent. Usually, the closer the relationship between the heir and the decedent, the lower the tax rate.

State and *federal income taxes* may also be due on income the deceased person earned during the last tax period before dying and on any income the estate earns while it is being administered. Tax will be due if the amount of either of these incomes exceeds the state and federal minimum limits.

If taxes are due, they may have to be paid (or prior consent obtained from the tax authorities) *before* the property can be distributed. All of the necessary tax forms and instruction booklets are available from the regional offices of the state and federal tax departments. The forms are not very complicated and, in most cases, the taxes are relatively simple to calculate. Both state and federal tax department employees can help you complete the forms and compute the taxes.

Substantial tax advantages can result from the manner and timing of tax payments and property transfers. This is particularly true for very large estates subject to federal estate tax. For these estates, consulting a tax expert or attorney may be advisable.

(4) Close the Estate

The personal representative must close probate as soon as possible — sometimes within a time limit set by state law. A form requesting the closing of the estate and release of the personal representative from further responsibility may have to be filed with the court. Some states also require a final accounting of the estate at this time.

Closing papers filed with the court by the personal representative must show that all required notices to interested persons were properly given; that the waiting period for the filing of claims against the estate was observed; that all valid claims against the estate and all expenses of administration have been paid; and that the necessary tax returns have been filed with the appropriate authorities.

If a final accounting is required, all that is necessary is a simple balance sheet that shows: (1) the estate's assets (the amount on the original inventory plus any assets discovered or received during administration); (2) the expenses of the estate (unpaid debts, creditors' claims, funeral expenses, court costs, professionals' fees, deductions, taxes, etc.); and (3) the resulting balance of the estate when expenses are subtracted from assets. The final account should also indicate how the estate's assets have been or will be distributed.

(5) *Distribute the Assets*

In some states, once the final account and closing papers have been filed, the personal representative must wait until the probate registrar completes an audit (checks the arithmetic of the final account). After the audit, the registrar's fees are paid, tax release forms are issued by the tax authorities and the remainder of the estate's assets are distributed.

Elsewhere, court supervision is less formal. The only requirement is that a final accounting be filed with the court so that interested persons can have an opportunity to raise objections. Property can be distributed without waiting if the personal representative is willing to risk the possibility of unforeseen claims. In states that permit unsupervised probate, no final court accounting is necessary unless some interested person asks for it.

A few states require that a report on the final distribution be filed with the court before the personal representative is released from responsibility. This report must include signed receipts from the *distributees* (those to whom assets were given) stating that they have received their shares of the estate. After closing probate, the personal representative should keep copies of all forms, receipts, expenses, claims, etc., in a personal file.

Conclusion

As you can see from this brief overview, probate consists chiefly of completing and filing standardized forms, listing estate assets, paying taxes and claims and disbursing assets to the heirs. Most of this can be accomplished by phone or mail.

The remainder of this manual explains the basic steps in greater detail, and the appendices give specific information about probate procedures and rules in all 50 states, the District of Columbia, the Virgin Islands and Puerto Rico. If you need further help, ask the staff in the office of the registrar of probate. You may also want to hire a lawyer or accountant for an hourly fee to advise you on specific technical matters.

Chapter 2

THE WILL

To open an estate for probate, you first need to know whether the decedent left a *will* (a written document directing how to distribute one's property after death). If a valid will exists (in which case the person is said to have died *testate*), you must submit it to the probate court in the county where the person legally resided. This is usually where the person lived a majority of the time, paid income taxes and was registered to vote. If no valid will exists (in which case the person died *intestate*), the estate must be probated and distributed according to state *laws of intestacy*.

The *personal representative* (the one responsible for probating the estate) will probably be named in the will, if one exists, but until a will can be found or shown not to exist, someone must take charge of searching for the will and then filing the appropriate papers with the probate court.

To prevent confusion in such cases, it is best for the family to name a member or friend to take charge temporarily. Ideally, this should be someone willing to act as personal representative once court approval has been obtained. Because they have personal knowledge of the estate, a surviving spouse or one of the children of the deceased is usually appointed to act as personal representative.

Probate With a Will

Whoever possesses the last will should give it to the personal representative named in the will or submit it to the probate court within 30 days of the death. If you don't know where the will is and you have agreed to assist with the estate, you should conduct a thorough search to find it.

Locating the Will

Check first with relatives and friends, then check the deceased person's files at home. If this turns up nothing, remember that some people file their wills with the probate registrar at the county courthouse, with their attorney, or in a safe-deposit box.

If you find that the will has been left with an attorney, remember that this places absolutely no obligation to hire that attorney to handle any or all of the probate process — *unless* the deceased person specified so in the will itself.

If the will is in a safe-deposit box, getting it is more complicated than simply taking it from the family safe. Call the bank and ask if anyone is familiar with the box's contents and how you can get the box opened for inspection. Many banks do not allow anyone to open a deceased person's safe-deposit box without *letters of administration* (discussed in Chapter 3.) Besides having these documents, it is often also required that a state tax representative be present to inventory the contents.

In some states, you need a court order to open a safe-deposit box. Other states have a simplified procedure for opening it if the only purpose is to check for a will. Of course, if the box was rented to two or more people and one of them is available, the process is even simpler. The bank can give you all the necessary details over the phone.

The state tax representative (usually the county treasurer or an assistant) may release the entire contents to you, including the will, if the items are mostly documents and sentimental possessions. If the box contains a great amount of cash or jewelry, you may have to get a consent form from the state tax authorities before you can get the valuables. In either case, inventory the box's contents so you can include them in your list of the assets of the estate.

Proving the Will

Once you have found a will, you must submit it to the probate court to be proved valid. This simply means establishing that the will is in fact the last will of the decedent and that it was executed according to the laws of the state in which the decedent legally resided.

In some states, a will may be accepted without further verification if it is *self-proved*. Although state requirements vary, a will is generally considered *self-proved* if it is executed according to state law and *notarized* at the time.

If the will is not self-proving, ask for *affidavit* forms from the registrar and use them to have the original witnesses attest to the validity of the will and signature. You should send the affidavit forms to the witnesses and include copies of the will and death certificate. Inform the witnesses that you intend to initiate probate, request that the affidavits be returned promptly, and remind them to have the affidavits notarized.

When the completed affidavits are returned to you or sent to the probate court, submit the will to the probate court along with any other forms you have completed (*e.g.*, applications to open the estate and for appointment as personal representative. See Chapter 3.) You can deliver the forms to the court personally or drop them in the mail, but be sure to make copies before you let anything out of your possession.

If the will was executed according to state law and no one contests its validity, no further formalities should be necessary. Some states may require a brief court hearing to prove the will. Some also may require the witnesses to be at the hearing to vouch for their affidavits. If the witnesses cannot be located or cannot attend the hearing, the court may require the testimony or affidavits of persons who can testify to the validity of the signatures of both the decedent and the witnesses.

Even if the will is not self-proving, you should have little difficulty in proving it or in initiating probate. The procedure is routine in most cases and even a court hearing involving witnesses rarely takes more than five minutes.

The Spouse's Right of Election

Most states allow the surviving spouse to choose between accepting the provisions of the will or receiving a fixed percentage of the estate regardless of the terms of the will. This *right of election* may be invoked *even if the will disinherits the spouse.* In fact, the procedure is designed to prevent attempts to disinherit spouses to ensure the spouse is not made destitute and dependent upon state aid. (See Appendix I.)

States that grant the right of election vary considerably with respect to the share of the estate the spouse can elect to receive. Some allow the spouse only a *life estate* interest in the deceased person's property. In these states, the spouse maintains a common law *right of dower* (for the wife) or the *right of curtesy* (for the husband) to use or live on one-third of the decedent's land for life. Other heirs may be entitled to own the land eventually, but they cannot receive or use that part of it while the spouse is alive.

Some states allow the surviving spouse to receive a special share of the estate's net value, while others simply allow the share that would pass to the spouse under the laws of intestacy if there were no valid will. A few states permit the spouse both to maintain life interest *and* to receive the share provided under intestacy laws.

The share the states allow the spouse under the right of election ranges from less than one-third of the estate to the entire estate, depending on circumstances. When a spouse exercises the right of election, the remaining heirs receive their share of the estate on a pro-rated basis. Refer to Appendix I and ask your probate registrar for the rules regarding the right of election in your state.

In addition to providing for election against the will, most states also grant a family allowance, a homestead exemption and/or a personal property allowance. These allowances shield money, the family home or the family's possessions from creditors or other beneficiaries. The amount and type of exemptions vary from state to state and can range between $1,000 and $20,000.

Probate Without a Will

A person who dies without having left a valid will is said to have died *intestate*. More than half of all estates entering probate are intestate.

State Intestacy Laws

Although the process is roughly the same throughout the country, each state has its own intestacy procedures. The intestacy laws that apply are those for the state in which the deceased person legally resided. If that person owned land in a second state, the laws of that state will govern distribution of the land located there.

To begin intestacy proceedings, you must submit an intestacy form to the probate court in place of a will. You can get the necessary form from the probate registrar. Send copies to all interested persons.

The court may then hold a hearing to name a personal representative to administer the estate. The appointment may be dictated by state law or the heirs may be allowed to name the personal representative. In some states, intestacy requires court-supervised administration of the estate (see Chapter 4). In others, probate can proceed without supervision once the personal representative has been appointed.

The most significant aspect of intestacy distribution is that all assets of the estate are totalled and treated equally for the purposes of distribution. The net value of the estate is divided proportionally among the heirs, with the share assigned each heir determined by his or her relationship to the deceased. The surviving spouse is usually entitled to a third to one-half of the estate, and the children of the deceased usually divide the rest equally. In some states, however, the spouse and children may be required to share the estate with other relatives. Appendix I lists the distribution requirements for each state.

Surveys have shown that intestacy laws seldom distribute assets the way most people would like to have their estate distributed. Nevertheless, for someone administering an intestate estate, the formula for distribution is clear and, in most cases, the distribution of assets will be no more difficult than had the person left a will.

The distribution requirements of intestacy laws can be waived if the heirs agree how to distribute the assets. Legal counsel may be advisable in such situations, but generally, distribution under intestacy laws is routine, whether the process is court-supervised or not. Two matters that do require special attention, however, are guardianship arrangements for minors and the handling of business and real estate interests.

Appointment of Guardians

Depending on the state, minor children of the deceased may inherit up to two-thirds of the estate under intestacy laws if there is a surviving spouse. If there is no surviving spouse, the children may inherit the entire estate. However, they cannot receive their shares until they reach the *age of majority* — either 18 or 21. The minor children's shares are held in trust by a court-appointed guardian until the children come of age.

In intestacy cases, a court hearing is usually held to name a guardian for minor children. In most estates that are covered by a will, guardians for minor children are named in the will. If not, they, too, must be appointed by the court. The closest kin, often the surviving spouse, is usually appointed to care for the children and manage their inheritances until they reach the age of majority. This official appointment may be required *even if the surviving spouse is also the natural parent of the children.*

Business and Real Estate Interests

If an owner or partner in a business dies without a will, some states require that the deceased person's share of the business be sold, even if all interested persons want to keep the business intact. It may also be necessary to sell some or all of any real estate the deceased person owned. In addition, business and real estate interests frequently have to be sold to satisfy the strict division of an estate required by intestacy laws. Usually, the sale of real estate or business interests must be approved in advance by the probate court.

Many states' intestacy laws favor *distribution in kind* instead of the forced liquidation of assets. This means, for example, that if a summer home was equal in value to a fourth of the total estate, a son entitled to a fourth of the estate might take the home instead of the cash equivalent of a fourth of the estate's total stocks, business interests, property, etc. If the heirs can agree on this sort of distribution, the family can avoid the forced sale of stocks, real estate or a business when prices are unacceptably low.

Will Contests

Those who want to contest a will must file an objection to the will in probate court within a specified number of days after the personal representative distributes the notice of probate. Any interested person — a legal heir, beneficiary or person with a declared interest in the estate — may question the validity of all or part of a will.

Will Contests and Questions

If a will contest succeeds, the person contesting the will receives that share of the estate he or she would get under intestacy laws. If the contest is over two or more existing wills, the contestants, if successful, are entitled to the shares given in the will established as valid. Until the contest is resolved, appraising the estate's assets and paying creditors may have to be postponed or turned over to a temporary manager.

A *contest* over all or part of a will should be distinguished from *questions* that courts frequently have to resolve. Such questions arise over the meaning of a will, the ownership of assets claimed by an estate, or the validity of claims or debts said to be owed by the person who dies. Will contests, on the other hand, challenge the *validity* of a will or one or more of its provisions.

Will contests must be started within definite time limits, while other forms of legal questions are not so strictly limited. Furthermore, clauses in a will that penalize heirs who contest the will frequently apply only to formal contests to the validity of all or part of a will, not to legitimate questions about the intentions of the deceased person.

Grounds for Contests

A will can be contested either on *procedural* grounds or on *substantive* grounds.

Procedural grounds exist if the will was improperly drawn, signed or witnessed. Each state has its own laws specifying how many witnesses must be present when the will is executed and what formalities must be followed. If two or more conflicting wills exist, the court must decide between them. This decision is usually based either on the execution dates (the most recently dated will revokes all previous wills), or on the testimony of witnesses.

The *substantive grounds* for contesting a will are more difficult to prove and rarely succeed. An example of a substantive ground is questioning the mental capacity of the deceased at the time the will was executed. A valid will requires only that the *testator* (the writer and signer of the will) be "of sound mind." "Sound mind" means that the testator knew the names of all persons who would be receiving property from the estate and understood the meaning of writing and executing a will.

Another substantive ground for contesting a will is "undue influence" — the use of force or duress to influence the terms of a will. This is also difficult to prove. Mere personal persuasive influence does not necessarily invalidate a will.

Unless settled by agreement of all interested persons, will contests must be resolved by court order after a formal court hearing. In a formal will contest, the personal representative is responsible for defending the presumed intent of the will against the claims of others. In most cases, the services of an attorney will be necessary if the contest goes to court. The attorney will be paid from the estate's assets, but this fee is separate from an attorney's fees for probating the estate.

Chapter 3
THE PERSONAL REPRESENTATIVE

The Uniform Probate Code (*UPC*, discussed in the "Conclusion" of this manual) uses the term *personal representative* (P.R.) to refer to the person responsible for administering a deceased person's estate. The term is intended to eliminate confusion that frequently arises from the traditional practice of using different terms depending on the *manner* in which the estate administrator is chosen.

States that adopted the term *personal representative* use it to replace *executor* and *executrix*, the masculine and feminine terms for the administrator of an estate *named in a will*. *Personal representative* also replaces *administrator* and *administratrix*, the masculine and feminine forms for an administrator *elected by the heirs* or *appointed by the court*.

Because the distinctions made by the traditional terms are of little practical value, this manual uses *personal representative* to refer to anyone responsible for administering an estate, regardless how chosen. You should be aware, however, that the other terms are still in standard use, as legalistic and confusing as they may be.

The Role of the P.R.

It is the personal representative's responsibility to initiate and complete probate, to inventory and distribute the estate's assets, to pay claims and taxes from the estate's funds, to engage whatever professional help is needed and generally to manage the affairs of the estate.

Selection of the P.R.

The person appointed personal representative is typically the surviving spouse, a relative or a friend of the deceased. Banks and corporate trust companies also can serve as personal representative, but it is seldom necessary to engage an expensive "expert" to handle the tasks involved. Most estates can be administered by anyone who can follow directions, add and subtract and ask questions, and a friend or relative will have the added advantage of being familiar with the last wishes and general estate affairs of the deceased.

If the person who died left a will, the personal representative is usually named in it. If the person named is unable or unwilling to serve, if no one is named in the will, or if the person died without a will, rules set by state law determine who can be named.

Under these conditions, the surviving spouse is usually entitled either to serve or to nominate someone else personal representative. In some states, the first heir to seek *letters of administration* may have priority for appointment.

When no surviving spouse is capable of administering the estate or nominating a substitute, the remaining heirs may make a nomination. The final selection must be approved in writing by all heirs. If no qualified person can be found, the heirs or the court may elect a corporate entity, such as a bank.

Opening the Estate

If you are named personal representative by a will, by the heirs or by the court, you must make an application to the probate court for an official appointment. The "application for appointment" form, available from the court and at most legal stationery stores, must be submitted to the probate registrar, usually along with the will. The registrar may also require a copy of the decedent's death certificate, an estimate of the estate's total value, and a list of the names and addresses of all known interested persons. The submission of these documents is called the "opening" of the estate.

Bonding Requirements

To protect the assets of the estate, you may be required by law to post a bond by paying a small fee.

Bonds insure against the loss of estate funds resulting from negligence or fraud by the personal representative.

In many states, this bond requirement can be waived by appropriate language in the will. Even if the will does state that bonding is not necessary, however, it can still be required if interested persons or the probate registrar request it. If bond is required, you can obtain it from bonding companies and agents, insurance companies or a bank. The cost of the bond premium can be deducted from the estate.

Serving Notice

The personal representative is responsible in some states for all notice requirements specified by state law. In other states, court personnel issue the required notices based on the information provided in the application to open the estate.

All interested persons must be notified of the person's death, of the opening of the estate for probate and of your application for appointment as personal representative. The legal requirements for notification vary from state to state, but they generally dictate the proper form for the notices, available from the court registrar's office; the method of delivery (in person or by first class, registered or certified mail); and the deadline for issuing each notice. Check Appendix I and ask your local probate registrar if you need more information about notice requirements.

Depending on the state, the personal representative or probate registrar is also responsible for notifying creditors that the estate is opening for probate. The notice must be published within a certain time after the opening.

Technically, notice to creditors is separate from notice to interested persons. As a practical matter, however, the two are frequently combined. It is often enough to publish the required number of times a single newspaper notice that announces the death, the opening of the estate and the application for appointment as personal representative.

In some states, mailing a copy of such a published notice to all known interested persons also serves as legal notification. As a matter of courtesy, known creditors should also be notified personally or by mail that the estate is being opened for probate. Appendix I tells you when these legal notices must be published.

Letters of Administration

The probate registrar should approve your application for appointment as personal representative soon after the required notices are published. The registrar will then open an official file for the administration of the estate and give you the personal representative's *letters of administration* (also called *letters testamentary*).

These letters are the official evidence of your authority to act on behalf of the estate. When you present them to persons who hold property of the deceased person or to officials responsible for transferring title to the property, those persons must immediately relinquish possession to you or transfer title to whomever is legally entitled to receive it.

Conclusion

Normally, no questions are raised about who will serve as personal representative or about the opening of the estate for probate. The entire process — applying for appointment, opening the estate and notifying creditors and interested persons — consists of routine formalities, all of which are often initiated at the same time. Approval of your application for appointment and giving you letters of administration then follow almost automatically.

Chapter 4

ESTATE ADMINISTRATION

You can probate an estate with one of three basic procedures: supervised, unsupervised and small-estate administration. As the names imply, supervised administration involves direct court supervision of all or part of the process, unsupervised administration has little court supervision and few formal reporting requirements, and small-estate procedures are used for estates valued at less than specified dollar limits set by state law.

The process you will have to use depends on the state in which probate occurs, the value of the estate and whether the person died with or without a will. If you live in a state that allows a choice between supervised and unsupervised administration, we strongly recommend you choose unsupervised administration because it involves considerably less paperwork and fewer trips to the courthouse.

If you are administering an estate that qualifies for small-estate administration, most formalities will be unnecessary. For more information on small-estate administration, see Chapter 13.

Supervised Administration

Supervised administration (also called *formal*, *solemn* or *regular* administration) requires court approval for some or all of the major steps in settling the estate. Although some states have added unsupervised procedures and others have reduced the amount of court supervision required, supervised administration is still the norm. Check Appendix I for your state's requirements.

In states that have both supervised and unsupervised procedures, you may be *required* to use supervised administration by the probate court or registrar. This is usually required if the one asking to be named personal representative does not appear to be qualified to handle unsupervised administration or if, after appointment, the personal representative seems to be administering the estate improperly.

Supervised probate involves completing various forms for submission to the court and a few informal court appearances, but it certainly is not beyond the abilities of most laypersons.

At most, fully supervised administration requires that you ask the court's approval at each step. You may have to submit preliminary and final estate inventories to the court, use court-approved appraisers, have the final inventory audited before you can pay debts or distribute the assets, verify payment of all debts and disbursements and swear to the accuracy of the accounts before the estate can be closed. None of these additional tasks is difficult. They are simply time-consuming.

The thing to remember about supervised administration is that any step in the probate process may require prior approval from the supervising probate court. You will simply have to make a point of asking the probate registrar which tasks require a return trip to the probate judge or registrar's office for approval.

Unsupervised Administration

Unsupervised administration (sometimes called *informal, independent, common* or *abbreviated administration*) involves a minimum of court supervision. The entire process is streamlined to simplify the role of the personal representative. The most common version is found in those states that have adopted the Uniform Probate Code (*UPC*). (See Appendix I.) Some other states allow unsupervised administration if it is authorized in the will, and still others have limited forms of unsupervised administration.

Basically, unsupervised administration does not free you from most of the tasks described in this manual. It does, however, free you from having to report to the probate court on each one. This makes unsupervised administration considerably quicker and easier for everyone.

If your state allows unsupervised administration, usually the written consent of all interested parties is enough to qualify for its use. The consent forms, which can be obtained from the probate registrar, must be filed with your application to open the estate. You should ask at this point if any other requirements have to be met and if other forms have to be completed to qualify for unsupervised administration.

In UPC states, the personal representative is responsible only to the heirs. Once the letters of administration have been issued, you usually are expected to settle and close the estate without further contact with the probate court.

In unsupervised administration, a published notice is usually not required to open the estate, nor for appointment of the personal representative. If, however, the heirs must choose the personal representative because it hasn't been taken care of in a will and there is no surviving spouse, the heirs' signed agreement to that choice must be filed with the opening papers.

You also still have to make an inventory of the deceased person's property, but it and the final accounting may be given to the heirs rather than filed with the court. Usually you also have to file with the court a short-form closing statement that all legal requirements have been met, but even this is not required in all states. Orders authorizing payment of claims and the final distribution of assets are also unnecessary under unsupervised procedures.

The use of informal procedures does not bar those interested from requesting court supervision. The UPC allows any interested person to ask the court to step in and go through formal procedures of proving a will is valid, to require that a final account be filed with the court or to supervise the distribution of the assets. After reviewing such a petition, the court may require supervision of the entire process or of only a particular aspect of administration.

In unsupervised administration, each stage of the process may be considered separately when questions are put before the probate court. For example, the formal proof of a will does not imply that the estate must be formally administered. Rather, it means the court is honoring a request that the witnesses to the will be asked to appear in court to testify that the will is authentic.

Ancillary Administration

A state's probate laws apply only to property physically located within its borders. Estates that include property outside the state of the decedent's legal residence (*ancillary property*) must be probated by a separate process. This is called ancillary administration.

This may be supervised or unsupervised, depending on the state in which the property is located. The important thing to remember about ancillary property is that, as personal representative, your ability to administer it may be limited. Some states will allow you to administer such property, but others will require that you name someone within the state (a *resident agent*) to receive correspondence and legal notices.

A few states even require that you name a separate personal representative living within the state to administer the ancillary property. This often results in the appointment of a local attorney or bank. If you must find a second personal representative to act in your behalf out-of-state, be sure to shop around and compare prices.

Chapter 5

ESTATE INVENTORY

The personal representative must complete an inventory of the estate within a specified time after it is opened. This period ranges from one to six months, depending on the state.

Although the inventory is intended for the court and interested parties, it is also useful to you as personal representative. It will help you prepare the final inventories the probate court asks you for, tax returns for the state and federal governments and the accounts needed to determine the correct distribution of the estate.

Probate and Non-Probate Assets

Some states require that only the probate assets of the estate be included in the estate inventory. Others insist that the inventory also include the non-probate assets.

Non-probate assets include most jointly-owned property and certain trusts, pensions and insurance benefits that have an individual specifically named as beneficiary. The *probate assets* may include any jointly-held property that is held without the right of survivorship. That is, if the deceased person's share of the property does not automatically pass to the surviving co-owner(s), that share is probably part of the probate estate.

In most states, the personal representative has no control over non-probate assets because they pass automatically to surviving beneficiaries or co-owners. However, you may be required to report the value of these assets for tax purposes. Also, some states base court fees and the fees allowed to the personal representative and probate attorney on the combined value of probate and non-probate assets.

Non-probate assets are discussed in Chapter 8. Although your inventory should separate non-probate and probate assets, the most important thing at this point is to correctly assess the value of each asset. If you have any questions about how to classify a particular asset, Chapter 8 should help you.

The Preliminary Estimate

Before completing a formal inventory and appraisal, a simple preliminary estimate of the value of the estate may be required when the estate is opened for probate. This estimate is particularly important if the estate can be shown to qualify for small-estate administration (Chapter 13).

The preliminary estimate can be useful in helping you organize your tasks and it will focus your attention on special needs of the estate. For example, it will help you calculate the cash needs of the estate (e.g., to pay utility bills) and determine whether or not you will have to sell any assets to raise the cash. The estimate also allows you to predict the overall tax impact on the estate and see if you will need the advice of a tax consultant.

Opening Estate Accounts

Before you begin seriously collecting and evaluating estate assets, it is essential that you realize the importance of keeping accurate financial records during the period of administration. One of the first things you should do as personal representative is open a bank account in the name of the estate. An interest-bearing checking account that can be drawn on by you will do fine.

All costs of estate administration should be paid from this account and all income deposited to it. Always remember to get receipts for money paid out and for assets sold or distributed.

If you establish an estate account at the start of probate, it will prove extremely helpful in completing the tax returns and the final accounting of the estate later on. It is also the best way to keep the estate's affairs orderly and separate from your own.

Searching for Assets

The formal inventory and appraisal of the estate begins with a thorough search for all assets. If you are unfamiliar with the estate's affairs, a person who was close to the decedent can probably describe and locate most assets. A few inquiries among relatives and friends can save you time and assure nothing is left out. You should also check personal papers and financial records for any evidence of unknown debts and assets. If the deceased person regularly employed a particular lawyer, that lawyer may have a summary of estate assets drawn up for estate planning.

Make a list of all estate assets as you locate them and indicate both the type of property (bank accounts, stock, vehicles, real estate, insurance policies, etc.) and the manner in which the property is owned (solely-owned or jointly-owned). All of the estate's assets should be listed in reasonable detail. Be sure to include the contents of any safe deposit boxes as well as registration numbers for all bank accounts, securities and insurance policies. It is also necessary to list all the person's debts (liens, mortgages, loans, outstanding balances on purchases, etc.) In the final inventory, list the probate and non-probate assets separately.

Valuing the Assets

The personal representative must appraise the value of all estate assets. These estimates are needed in order to account for the worth of the entire estate, to determine the estate's tax liabilities and to establish the value of each beneficiary's share.

Each state varies in its requirements for estate appraisals. Typically, real estate and personal property must be appraised separately and by different methods. Unless the probate court orders otherwise, you can determine the value of most personal property yourself. Real property (real estate) and other items of great value may have to be appraised by a professional appraiser. The probate registrar can tell you if the services of a professional appraiser are required.

Appraisal by Personal Representative

To determine the value of bank accounts, simply check the balances with the bank in which they are held. Stocks and bonds can be valued by checking the stock listings in a daily newspaper and assigning stock shares a value midway between the "high" and "low" value listed for the date of the person's death. (Remember that stock listings in newspapers are usually for the day before the date of publication.) Most furniture and household goods can be appraised in a lump sum, based on a reasonable "garage sale" price. Items of special value, however, should be listed and valued separately.

Professional Appraisers

You may employ a professional appraiser to help value some or all of the assets, but make sure this is not someone with an interest in the estate. In many states, the court will appoint a professional appraiser or require you to hire one privately to value assets such as real estate, antiques, valuable jewelry and other items of value.

Depending on state and local court rules, even the smallest items may have to be listed and valued separately on your inventory. In such cases, the cost of a professional appraiser may be considerable. If the court does not impose a particular appraiser on you, be sure to shop around for competitive prices. You should also attend all on-sight appraisals.

If you employ a professional to assess the value of the estate, the name and address of the appraiser should appear on the inventory. The appraiser's fee may be paid from estate funds on receipt of the completed and signed appraisals. Be sure to obtain a receipt for the final inventory and for your records.

Tax Consequences

All property of the estate must be valued as of the date of death. The one exception is for large estates (more than $500,000 in 1986, $600,000 in 1987 and years after) when calculating federal estate taxes. The federal estate tax allows you to choose between valuing the estate at the date of death or six months after that date. The latter date may be advantageous if property or stock values depreciate substantially during the six months. Large estates with many investment assets frequently have widely fluctuating values, but remember that all items must be valued as of the same date. Get a copy of IRS publication 448 from your regional IRS office to help determine whether or not the alternative date can decrease the estate's tax liability.

The appraisal of the estate's assets will have an influence on the tax that will be due on the property and may also influence how much the beneficiaries will receive. Since probate involves paying taxes as well as transferring property, you should check the state and, if necessary, federal tax tables when you know the approximate value of the estate. If you expect a significant tax impact on the estate, you may want to seek professional tax advice.

Looking at the tax tables and forms at this point also can be of considerable help in completing the inventory and appraisal. Because you must file tax returns in any case, it can save you a lot of time if you begin collecting the information for the returns while conducting the inventory. This not only helps you organize the administration of the estate, it also expedites the clearance from the tax authorities that may be required to transfer title to property, distribute shares to beneficiaries, or close the estate. It's worth noting that in some states you can even use the completed tax form to satisfy the inventory and appraisal requirements of both the probate court and the state tax authorities. However, don't file the tax returns until you know the value of all claims and expenses of administration, because these can be deducted from the taxable estate.

All property appraisals must be based on a fair market price, but remember that any item has a wide range of "reasonable" values. For tax purposes, the lowest reasonable assessment may not always be the most advantageous, particularly if valuable property may be sold by you or other heirs after the estate is distributed. Personal income tax rates are generally higher than inheritance tax rates. A higher initial valuation may mean that an heir will pay higher inheritance tax but will avoid paying still higher income taxes on the difference between the probate appraisal price and the sale price when the property is sold.

Assuming Possession of Property

As you proceed with the inventory, you should take possession of all probate assets of the estate, unless you have good reason not to do so — if, for example, it is in the hands of someone who can properly manage the property or someone who will ultimately receive it anyway. Collect all valuables, contents of safe deposit boxes, bank accounts, securities, income and other money owed to the decedent or the estate.

If estate funds are available, you may have to pay some debts to release property being held as collateral. You should also file claims for any insurance or other benefits that are due the estate and make sure all individual beneficiaries of policies file claims of their own.

As personal representative, you are the legal custodian of all probate assets of the estate and personally responsible for them. When you present the personal representative's letters of administration, all probate property should be released to you promptly by the person holding it or responsible for transferring its title. If you encounter any difficulty, you can get a special court order to present with the letters of administration.

When the final inventory and appraisal are completed, file a copy with the probate court if that is required. In any event, definitely send a copy to all interested persons.

Chapter 6

CREDITORS' CLAIMS

When a person dies, usually bills remain to be paid — medical and funeral expenses, ongoing rent and utility bills. Settling such bills involves a simple procedure. It begins with publication of a notice in a local newspaper informing creditors that the person has died and the estate is being opened for probate. Your state's specific requirements for the notice, including the number of times it must be published, will be explained by the probate registrar.

Once probate has begun, creditors can present their claims directly to you as personal representative or to the probate court. In some states, all claims must be filed with the court. Creditors' claims must state the basis of the claim, the amount and the date due, and the name and address of the person claiming payment.

Collect All Claims

The personal representative is responsible for listing all claims and all bills owed. Most will be from routine monthly charges mailed directly to the person's home — rent and utilities, for example. A monthly billing statement sent to the home address of the deceased is usually considered a valid claim. Other bills you can expect are those that result from a last illness and funeral arrangements.

You should also check personal papers and financial records to determine if there are other creditors and notify banks at which the deceased person may have had an outstanding loan. After the waiting period for submitting claims has expired, check if any claims have been filed with the probate court.

Evaluate Each Claim

When you have collected all bills and claims, examine each one to determine if it is valid, reasonable and accurate. If you are not satisfied that a particular claim is valid, you must mail a *notice of disallowance* to the creditor within a certain time after the deadline for submitting claims. The notice may disallow part of a claim or deny all of it. In response, the creditor must either accept your rejection of the claim or apply to the court to allow it. The creditor must do this within a certain number of days after receiving your disallowance notice.

Elaborate exchanges between the personal representative, creditors and the probate court are extremely rare and are unlikely to pose difficulties. If problems do arise, check with the probate registrar about the specific details of the various notices and time periods required by state law.

Pay Valid Claims

In a few states, you must get court approval before paying any claims or bills. In most states, however, you need court permission only to pay large claims. Generally, if cash is available in the estate's bank account, you can use these funds to pay routine bills. Valid claims filed with the court or found in the deceased person's records should be paid when the waiting period for the submission of all claims has expired. Make the payments *after* receiving court approval, if that approval is necessary.

Occasionally, estates lack enough assets to pay all of the debts and the expense of administering the estate. In such cases, check with the probate registrar about arranging any necessary family living allowances and the payment of *preferred claims*.

Preferred claims are those that must, by state law, be paid before others and before the assets are distributed among the heirs. They often include charges for funeral services and fees for the personal representative and attorney, if there was one. (See Chapter 10 on "Fees" and Appendix I, and ask the probate registrar for further details.) The remaining claims against the estate can be paid on a pro-rated basis after payment of the preferred claims.

If the inventory shows that the estate has too little cash to cover its debts, the beneficiaries may have to choose between contributing cash and accepting the forced sale of assets. This frequently occurs when the assets are mostly in real estate and an injection of cash by all beneficiaries is preferred to selling valuable real estate at an inopportune time. (Real estate sales are discussed in the next chapter.)

Sometimes a creditor will fail to file a claim within the allotted time. This technically means the claim is barred. You are under no legal obligation to pay such claims, but most people are reluctant not to pay them if they are valid. If you are confronted with a late claim like this and decide to pay it, first get the consent of the *residuary beneficiaries*, those who will receive the remainder of the estate after the specified inheritances and other expenses have been paid.

It is extremely unlikely that you will face any of the problems described above. In fact, creditors rarely read the notices in the newspapers or come forward to file claims against an estate. More typically, the estate will be confronted only with routine monthly billings and established debts that are familiar to the deceased person's family.

Chapter 7

REAL ESTATE SALES

Most estates include a home that must either be transferred or sold during probate. For example, you may have to sell land or buildings to raise cash for taxes and claims, or to distribute the shares of the estate, whether those shares are dictated by a will or by state intestacy laws.

Selling real estate involves placing the property on the market, negotiating offers and perhaps mortgage arrangements, transferring title and settlement closings. In most cases, this requires the services of banks, real estate brokers and appraisers and lawyers. The entire process and tips for dealing with real estate professionals are described in HALT'S *Citizens Legal Manual,* **Real Estate**. Refer to that manual before proceeding with the sale of any property.

Probate-Related Problems

Selling real estate during probate is more complicated than selling other assets. Usually, you are not allowed to sell any real estate until a specified time after the estate is opened for probate. You may also need the approval of both the court and the deceased person's spouse.

Selling real estate during probate also involves a few considerations not explained in HALT's **Real Estate** manual. For example, the existence of homestead and "set aside" laws in some states can prevent the sale of a family home as long as the surviving spouse and minor children need to use it, regardless of the estate's need for cash to pay bills or provisions in the will. Ask the probate registrar to explain your state's laws regarding homestead exemptions.

Real Estate Fees

Professional fees for real estate sales are another major concern. The sale of real property will bring large amounts of cash into the estate. This may unnecessarily increase the value of the probate estate, the number often used in calculating fees for the estate's lawyer and personal representative. Some states exclude real estate (even solely-owned property) when calculating probate fees, *unless the property is sold.* Once it is sold, you can expect the lawyer's and personal representative's fees to jump proportionately. Also, the real estate broker will collect a commission, further adding to the cost of probate. For these reasons, it may be best to avoid selling real estate during probate if at all possible.

A further caution: if you hire a lawyer to administer the estate and real property must be sold, be warned that it is a common practice for the lawyer to engage a broker for the sale. Sometimes lawyers agree to pay the broker the current market rate (5 to 8 percent of the property's value), then charge the estate 10 percent, pocketing the extra themselves even if they did no work on the sale.

If you must sell real estate during probate, investigate both the legal maximum and the current market rates for brokers' commissions and make sure the estate is charged a competitive price, not simply the maximum allowed by the law.

Beneficiaries often prefer to receive "in kind" inheritances instead of real estate. This type of distribution — and the problems it may pose for the personal representative — are discussed in the sections on "Business and Real Estate Interests" in Chapter 2 and "Testate Distribution" in Chapter 12.

Chapter 8
PROPERTY TRANSFERS

Almost all estates include assets that can be transferred directly to the surviving spouse or other heirs without going through probate. These assets are generally not subject to probate fees and costs, and their transfer need not be delayed until the estate is closed.

Because the transfer of non-probate assets falls outside the normal probate process, a substantial amount of time and money may be saved for the estate and heirs by avoiding the normal court costs, lawyers' fees and inevitable delays. However, it is important to realize that non-probate assets are *not* exempt from taxation nor from the claims of creditors if the estate's probate assets are not sufficient to cover its debts.

Several forms of property ownership can prevent assets from being included in the probate estate. Some advantages may be gained by using property forms that avoid probate, but only a carefully balanced estate plan can benefit an estate. Some probate-avoidance mechanisms are simple to create and maintain, such as joint tenancy. Others, such as living trusts, require careful management of assets and special tax returns each year. These tax and management considerations should be kept in mind when weighing the advantages of avoiding probate.

For a full explanation of estate planning techniques and probate-avoidance ownership strategies, see HALT's *Citizens Legal Manual*, **Estate Planning**. Such strategies are of more concern to the decedent and heirs *before* death than they are to the personal representative after probate begins, but because the administration of most estates involves the transfer of some non-probate assets, this chapter gives a brief explanation of the various forms of property ownership and how to handle their transfers.

Classifying Assets

Dividing estate property accurately between probate and non-probate assets is not always simple. Assets owned by both the deceased and one or more other persons may or may not involve survivorship rights. In some states, the answer will depend upon whether the ownership registration mentions survivorship or "joint tenancy." In several states, all assets jointly registered to a married couple are *automatically* survivorship property, even if title to the property or the account registration does not mention survivorship, "joint tenancy" or the marital status of the co-owners.

Determining the ownership of jointly-registered bank accounts is often complicated by local laws. Life insurance benefits are also subject to various death taxes, as are survivors' rights in employee benefits that include joint and survivor annuities.

If in doubt, ask about the type of ownership and the tax status of estate assets by contacting the banker, securities agent or insurance agent involved. Staff at the probate registrar's office may also be willing to help you classify assets. However, court personnel are usually reluctant to give such advice "over-the-counter" because they do not want to assume responsibility for questions that cannot be answered quickly and accurately.

If you can't determine the legal status of an asset that accounts for a large part of the estate's net worth, you should probably get a lawyer's advice. It shouldn't take long for an attorney to give you an answer, and an hour of the attorney's time may be worth the savings to the estate.

Joint Tenancy

As with probate assets, non-probate assets fall into two categories: real property (land and permanent structures) and personal property (furniture, bank accounts, insurance, stocks and bonds, personal effects, etc.) The most common way such assets are held is in some form of joint ownership with rights of survivorship, although most insurance policies, trusts, public and private pensions and other death benefits are also considered non-probate assets.

Property jointly-owned by two or more persons with rights of survivorship generally is transferred "automatically" to the surviving owners. The transfer is made without probate and without regard to any provisions of the will. The "right of survivorship" is the right of all co-owners to assume the share of any owner who dies. The exact wording of the title to jointly-owned property will control the manner in which the property is transferred.

In most states, using the words *joint tenants* or *joint tenancy* in the title of ownership is enough to assure that the surviving owners receive the property when a co-owner dies. The formal phrase describing this common form of joint-ownership is *joint-ownership with the right of survivorship*. Use of this phrase is required in some states to make a non-probate transfer possible. A similar form of joint ownership — with the significant exception that its use is limited to married couples — is called *tenancy by the entirety*.

Although most jointly-owned property passes "automatically" to the surviving owners, a few simple formalities must be completed. Typically, this involves deleting the name of the deceased owner from the title, deed, certificate or other record of ownership and getting a new document registered solely in the names of the surviving owners.

Each surviving co-owner is entitled to receive an equal share of the deceased owner's interest in the jointly-owned property unless the original ownership document states otherwise. If the property was jointly owned by two owners, the surviving co-owner becomes sole owner of the property.

In many states, to transfer such property to a surviving owner or owners, you must present several documents to the official responsible for transferring title. These documents vary from state to state and depend on the nature and form of ownership, but typically they include the following:

- A certified copy of the death certificate.
- A declaration or notarized affidavit stating that the co-owners have a right to the jointly-owned property.

- A consent-to-transfer form (or release of inheritance tax lien) from state and, if necessary, federal tax authorities. That is, you must show the estate has sufficient assets to cover debts and taxes.
- A new deed (for real property) stating the survivors' names exactly as they appear in the old deed.
- An appraisal of the property's value which, in many states, can be the most recent value assigned by the state tax assessor. Otherwise, a professional appraiser's assessment may be required.
- A verification of your signature.
- A nominal transfer and registration fee.

Not all of these materials will be required for all assets in all states. Once you have obtained and completed the necessary forms and have gathered any other required information, you need only present it to the proper official in person or by mail.

For real property, you may have to present all of the above forms to the recorder of deeds in the county where the deceased person legally resided. You should also send copies to the recorders of deeds in the counties where the property is located. For other property, such as jointly-owned stock certificates and bank accounts, you may only need to present a death certificate, a declaration of co-ownership, a consent-to-transfer form from the tax authorities and a small fee.

In some states, you may even be able to complete the transfer with a simple *termination of joint-ownership* form at the probate registrar's office. This can be sent by you or the registrar to the proper officials to obtain the release of property. A few phone calls to the probate registrar, the recorder of deeds, a bank or a broker should yield all the forms and information you need.

In general, registering property in joint tenancy or in trust is enough to authorize a direct non-probate transfer to those legally entitled to receive the property. (Trusts are discussed later in this chapter.) If the person claiming the property is a surviving spouse, complications and difficulties rarely occur. If you encounter any difficulty with financial institutions or public officials responsible for transferring title to jointly-owned property, discuss it with the probate registrar or, if necessary, with a lawyer.

Community Property

Community property is recognized by the laws of eight states — Arizona, California, Idaho, Louisiana, Nevada, New Mexico, Texas and Washington. In these states, all property owned by a married couple is considered "community property." This includes all property acquired *during* marriage that was not a gift or inheritance to one spouse or specifically kept separate. The earnings of both spouses and any property derived from those earnings are both considered community property. In some states, income earned by separate property (for example, income from rental housing owned by one spouse) is *also* community property.

Unlike joint ownership, community property *does not include any right of survivorship.* When one spouse dies, the survivor owns only his or her share of the community property — in most cases, half of all the earnings and property acquired by both spouses during the marriage.

The share owned by the spouse who died can be transferred by his or her will (or by state intestacy laws) to the surviving spouse or to some other person. The deceased spouse's share must usually be probated, although this varies from state to state. (California, for example, has abolished probate for property that passes directly from one spouse to the other.) Some states even allow the spouse a choice of whether or not to probate all or part of the community property. In such cases, the surviving spouse should weigh the advantages and disadvantages of going through probate.

Half of the community property owned by the spouse who died must be included in the gross estate for calculating estate or inheritance taxes.

Trusts

A trust can be used either in conjunction with or in place of a will. It is generally used to avoid probate and to provide for the competent management of assets on behalf of the *donor* (the creator of the trust) and the *beneficiaries* (those for whom the trust is created). The person or institution named by the donor to manage the trust is called a *trustee*.

In a typical simple trust, parents place their assets in a special account to be managed by a relative or financial institution for the benefit of their children's education. Trusts also commonly name the donors of the trust (for example, a husband and wife) as joint trustees and/or beneficiaries. This usually takes the assets out of the control of probate court. Trusts can also help large estates reduce estate taxes when those who create the trust do not retain any rights to use or control the assets placed in the trust.

The type of trust determines whether or not the assets placed in it will have to be probated. The two most common types are the *testamentary trust* (established by the provisions of a will) and the *living* or *inter vivos trust* (established during the lifetime of the donor.)

A testamentary trust is subject to probate because it is set up as part of a will. The assets in such a trust must be distributed in probate according to the terms of the will. At the closing of the estate, as personal representative you must transfer the assets assigned to the trust to the appointed trustee, and the trustee must manage and distribute the assets according to the terms spelled out in the will.

Living trusts can be either *revocable* or *irrevocable*. As the terms imply, revocable living trusts can be altered or completely revoked at any time during the life of the donor, and irrevocable living trusts cannot be altered or revoked unless an alteration or termination date is specified in the trust arrangement itself.

Revocable living trusts are the most widely used trust forms. One reason is that they avoid probate. They have the additional advantage of allowing the donor to control the assets in the trust until his or her death. However, since the donor maintains control of the assets, they remain within the gross estate and are subject to estate taxes.

Irrevocable living trusts are usually outright gifts that are to be given to a beneficiary by the appointed trustee after the donor dies. The gift can be given in a lump sum at a specified date or in installments, depending on the terms specified by the donor. In general, irrevocable trusts pass completely out of the control of the donor, but if a termination date is included in the trust agreement, the donor can decide at that time whether to take back control of the assets or extend the trust.

Irrevocable living trusts traditionally were used to gain estate tax savings, but changes in federal gift and estate tax laws have eliminated some of those savings. Nevertheless, both revocable and irrevocable trusts that give income for life to the donor's children and the remaining assets to grandchildren can still, within limits, save some estate taxes, and the careful use of trust arrangements can obtain other, if less dramatic, tax savings.

Living trusts, both revocable and irrevocable, transfer the title to assets before the donor dies. Thus, they need not be transferred during probate because they do not technically belong to the donor, even if the donor is also a trustee and the beneficiary is the donor's spouse. As personal representative, you have no responsibility for the assets placed in a living trust and need only be aware of them for general accounting and taxation purposes.

Death Benefits

Death benefits from insurance policies and pension plans are generally exempt from probate, provided that the policies name a beneficiary who survives the owner of the policies. Once the appropriate claim forms are filed by the personal representative or the beneficiary, the benefits can be paid directly to the named beneficiaries.

Death benefits from life insurance policies also frequently escape state inheritance taxes, but there is no comparable exemption from federal estate taxes. The tax consequences of benefits due under various retirement plans vary greatly, so it's best to consult directly with the company that administers the pension plan.

One of the first things you should do as personal representative or as surviving spouse is to search the deceased person's files and personal papers for insurance policies and pension plan records. If you know the names of the insurance companies or agents, you can ask them for copies of all the decedent's policies (life, disability, property, automobile, etc.)

The insurance company can also help you complete the claim forms, and many will even help you complete the tax forms required for the insurance benefits, including IRS Form 712, which must be filed with any federal estate tax return if insurance benefits are being collected.

The only difficulty you may encounter with collecting on a life insurance policy is if it names the estate as beneficiary, or if no individual is named. Insurance companies are extremely hesitant to pay benefits to anyone not specifically named in the policy. Those policies that assign benefits to the estate or that are vague about who should be the beneficiaries must be probated.

When checking insurance policies, you may find it necessary to increase the coverage on some property policies to bring them into line with new appraisals. Conversely, it may be necessary to cancel others if they are no longer of use. Policies on jointly-owned property that has passed to surviving owners should be cancelled or registered under the survivors' names.

Other Benefits

Besides insurance benefits, heirs may also be due benefits from company or private retirement plans, Social Security, the Veterans Administration, credit unions or other sources. Specifically, Social Security may provide survivors' benefits to the spouse and minor children as well as a death benefit to help cover funeral expenses. Benefits due from Social Security must be claimed through the deceased person's local Social Security office.

Always check with the deceased person's employer about additional company benefits. For example, the person may have been involved in a company profit-sharing plan. And, of course, you should ask about workers' compensation for work-related deaths. Check also with other private companies, unions or fraternal organizations that may owe benefits to the deceased person or survivors.

Chapter 9

TAXES

Paying state and federal taxes, although technically separate from probate procedures, is nevertheless part of the personal representative's responsibilities.

Taxes are due on the whole estate, not only the assets subject to probate. The taxes must be computed and the returns filed, usually with tax authorities, during administration of the estate. The assets often cannot be distributed until all taxes have been paid or until the tax authorities have given permission by issuing a consent-to-transfer.

The personal representative is responsible for completing and filing the tax returns for the estate. At first glance, this can appear to be highly technical, involving completion of as many as six different forms: state and federal income tax returns for the decedent, state and federal income tax returns for the estate, a state inheritance or estate tax return and a federal estate tax return. A quick look at the lengthy federal estate tax return alone is enough to send some people flying into the arms of the nearest professional accountant or lawyer.

Intimidating as they may seem, however, you can handle the tax returns for most estates quickly and easily. Only very large estates with fairly complicated assets should require the services of a professional tax advisor. The state tax returns are usually short and simple forms that come with detailed instructions. They are no more complex than your state's personal income tax forms.

The dreaded federal estate tax, with its long and complicated forms, applies to only an extremely few estates, and even these forms are not as difficult as they first appear. Also, the probate registrar and the staff of state and federal tax offices, though not intended as substitutes for professional tax consultants, can answer basic questions about taxes and forms.

The remainder of this chapter (and Appendix II) surveys the types and amounts of taxes that may be due on the estate you are administering. Further information about taxes, exemptions, deductions and tax credits can be found in government publications available from state and federal tax offices. Be sure to check all tax information against the most current publications of tax authorities because the figures and allowances change frequently — particularly state-tax rates.

Personal Income Taxes

The rules governing personal income taxes apply equally to all income earned during the tax year in which a person dies. All a deceased person's income above the allowed exemptions during the year of his or her death is taxable for that year. For example, if an unmarried person died in June, 1986, after earning more than $3,300 in that year, the personal representative for the estate must file a federal *personal income tax return* for the amount earned, less deductions.

A state income tax return may also have to be filed. The tax rates, forms and due dates are the same as for personal state income taxes, and the taxes must be paid to the appropriate tax authorities, not the probate court. For further information, call your regional IRS office and request a copy of IRS Publication 559, *Tax Information for Survivors, Executors and Administrators*.

Estate Income Taxes

An estate becomes a taxable entity in its own right upon the death of its owner. The personal representative must file an *estate income tax return* with state and federal governments if the income earned by the estate in any tax year exceeds the standard exemptions. That is, if the estate's gross income exceeds the tax-exempt minimum in any January-December period during the estate's administration, a return must be filed. Because probate often requires a year or longer to complete, many estates do earn income, for example from stock dividends or rents. As with personal income taxes, the estate's income tax return and payment must be made to the IRS and state tax authorities, not the probate court. The proper form for the federal estate income tax is the U.S. Fiduciary Income Tax Return, IRS Form 1041. You can get it from your regional IRS office.

Call the IRS as soon as possible after opening the estate for probate and ask for whatever federal tax forms you may need. Be sure to ask also for a *federal estate tax identification number*. This number must be used if you are required to file either the federal estate income tax form or the federal estate tax form.

You can get information and forms regarding *state estate income taxes* from your state's tax authorities or, in many cases, from the probate registrar.

State Inheritance and Estate Taxes

Every state except Nevada imposes some form of "death tax." The taxes are assessed either as an *inheritance tax* on each heir's share of the estate, or as an *estate tax* on the total value of the estate. A few states require no state tax return unless a federal estate tax return is also required. (See "Credit Estate Tax" discussed below.)

The amount of state *inheritance tax* that must be paid depends on the relationship of an heir to the deceased person. Inheritances received by spouses, children and grandchildren, for example, are usually taxed at a lower rate than those received by brothers and sisters, while other beneficiaries are taxed at a higher rate. Personal exemptions from these inheritance taxes often apply. These vary for different heirs in different states.

The personal representative is usually responsible for calculating and arranging payment for inheritance taxes. Unlike other taxes discussed in this chapter, these often must be filed with the probate court rather than the tax authorities. Ask your probate registrar.

Some wills specifically ask the personal representative to pay inheritance taxes from estate funds before distributing the assets. Alternatively, state law may require such advance payment. There is no firm rule on who pays these taxes. It may be the personal representative or the heirs. Your probate registrar can tell you what is required in your area.

A few states impose a *state estate tax*. As with the federal estate tax, this is based on a graduated percentage of the *total* value of the estate. For this tax, the relationship of the heir and the deceased is irrelevant, as there is only one tax schedule and usually only one exemption — for the estate as a whole. In states that use an *estate tax*, the personal representative must file and pay it to the appropriate tax authority.

Each state, whether it imposes an inheritance tax or an estate tax, uses a different tax-rate schedule and has different allowances for personal exemptions. Contact the tax authorities in the state in which the deceased person lived to get the necessary forms and instruction booklets.

In most states, computing, filing and paying state taxes is a simple "do-it-yourself" task, although in some states a state tax referee or a brief court hearing may be required to determine how much tax is due. Some states may also require that you include copies of several documents with your state tax returns: (1) the will, (2) an inventory and appraisal of the estate, (3) a court-approved application to open the estate for probate and (4) payment of the amount due.

Credit Estate Tax

Some states impose a special tax, usually called a *credit estate tax*, on estates that have to pay the *federal estate tax* (*i.e.*, estates above $500,000 in 1986, above $600,000 in years after). In some states, this credit estate tax is the only state tax. In others, it is in addition to either the inheritance tax or the estate tax.

The federal estate tax law allows large estates a standard credit (*i.e.*, a reduction in the tax owed) for payment of state inheritance or estate taxes. In turn, many states tax the estate the amount of the allowed federal credit. In effect, it amounts to a federal government tax "rebate" to the state.

State and federal tax information booklets explain how the credit is determined for the different sizes and categories of estates.

Federal Estate Tax

The personal representative can determine whether or not a *federal estate tax return* must be filed by computing the total value of the *gross estate* (everything the decedent owned or had an interest in or that is owed the estate). If the value is greater than $500,000 in 1986 or $600,000 in years after, a federal estate tax return must be filed within nine months of the decedent's death. This is true even if the allowable exemptions, deductions and tax credits erase any tax liability. In fact, after applying the various deductions and tax credits allowed to most estates, many estates do end up having to file a return without having to pay a tax.

If the estate must pay federal estate taxes, it may be best to consult a competent tax advisor. Determining federal estate tax exemptions and deductions can be the most difficult part of estate administration, and a good tax consultant can save a large and complicated estate enough taxes to compensate for the fees that will be charged.

Remember to use your *federal estate tax identification number* with your return and, if taxes are due, be sure to include full payment. If the estate cannot afford to pay all of the tax at once, a special 10-year payment schedule with reasonable interest rates can be arranged.

For further information about federal estate taxes, the federal marital deduction and the federal gift tax, call your regional IRS office and ask for a copy of IRS Publication 448, *Federal Estate and Gift Taxes*.

Chapter 10

PROBATE FEES

The personal representative and the attorney for the estate, if there is one, are both entitled to compensation from the estate for their services in conducting probate. The amounts of their fees, however, are regulated by state laws and the probate court.

Generally, personal representatives who are friends or members of the family of the deceased person do not collect fees from the estate, or collect only nominal amounts for their services, but if a bank, trust company or other corporation is named personal representative, or if a probate attorney is retained by the family or the court to administer the estate as personal representative, these fees can take a large bite out of the estate.

To protect estates from exorbitant charges, laws establish an absolute maximum or "reasonable" limit on the size of fees. These limits are supposedly allowed only for administering the most difficult estates. In practice, however, the maximum fees have become a license — particularly for lawyers and corporate personal representatives — to charge the maximum allowable for virtually all estates. Most probate lawyers charge these fees without regard for the actual services rendered or the time or skill required, and the courts routinely endorse these maximum charges as "customary" fees. When converted to hourly rates, they can mean the estate is paying as much as $1,000 an hour for simple administrative and clerical tasks.

Percentage Fees

In some states, the "maximum" fee for both the personal representative and lawyer combined is based on a percentage of the value of the estate. This percentage varies from state to state and is frequently measured on a sliding scale, for example: 10 percent of the first $20,000 of an estate's value, 4 percent of the next $50,000, etc. These "maximum" fees *do not* include additional charges for "extraordinary services" lawyers or corporate personal representatives decide are needed.

The law generally requires that such percentage fees be based on the value of the *probate estate* — the total assets collected and distributed by the personal representative, excluding those that pass to heirs outside of probate. However, fees are often illegally based on the value of the *gross estate* — everything the deceased owned at death. This practice often greatly increases a lawyer's or personal representative's fee.

Whether the percentage fees are based on the probate estate or the gross estate, HALT opposes them as an arbitrary and ridiculous way to calculate how much should be paid for probate work. For example, $100,000 worth of stock in a corporation can be transferred to an heir with no more time, effort or risk than $100 worth of the same stock. The transfer can be made by anyone who can make a phone call or write a letter. Yet a lawyer or corporate personal representative can ask a fee 1,000 times higher for the larger transaction, even though in both cases the transfer is probably performed by a lawyer's legal secretary or paralegal.

'Reasonable' Fees

Some states have replaced the percentage limit on fees with a law that allows lawyers to charge a "reasonable fee" but keeps in place the percentage-fee system for personal representatives. Other states require both lawyers and personal representatives to charge a "reasonable fee," and the rest have no provisions regarding lawyers' fees. (See Appendix I.)

The shift from the percentage limit to a "reasonable" standard is intended to require lawyers to base their fee requests on the work actually performed, the time and skill required for the work and customary local charges for such work. The "reasonable" standard is an improvement over the percentage system because it allows the personal representative and heirs an opportunity to challenge fee requests and demand some justification for the charges.

The "reasonable" standard has not, however, eliminated the fee problem. A review of probate legal bills reveals that "reasonableness" is often equated with the maximum percentage of the estate's value allowed (or previously allowed) for the personal representative. State probate codes seldom give clear definitions of what is "reasonable" and seldom require itemized fee requests. As a result, probate courts tend to accept the traditional practice of basing fees on the size of the estate rather than the complexity of the work involved.

Lawyers' Fees

When probate fees must be approved by the court, heirs often believe they'll be protected by the court and won't be overcharged. Consequently, they fail to protect themselves by getting a written fee agreement with a lawyer *before* services are provided.

If you are the personal representative for an estate and decide to hire a lawyer to help you, take steps to ensure that the lawyer's fees will be based on the actual work done. To do this, you need a written agreement signed by both you and the lawyer. It should state clearly that fees will be computed on an hourly basis for specific services rendered.

The fee arrangement between the personal representative and the lawyer for the estate must be made separately from any arrangement provided for in the will. Because old wills may contain unreasonably low fee provisions, state laws generally allow personal representatives and lawyers to choose between the provisions made for fees in the will and the guidelines established by state law.

Remember, however, that a state's percentage maximum or reasonable-fee standard does not mean that you are required by law to pay those amounts to an attorney. They are only maximum limits. You can negotiate a contract with a lawyer that specifies an hourly rate, instead. In fact, it will probably mean substantial savings for the estate if you do.

Hiring a Lawyer

If you do decide to hire a lawyer, you have two options regarding the type of service you buy and the fee arrangement you make with the lawyer.

The first is to hire the lawyer to administer every aspect of probate. Technically, this is not the proper way to conduct probate. As personal representative, *you* are the one responsible for administering the estate and distributing its assets. The lawyer is only there to help with the tasks involved and to ensure that everything you do is technically correct. However, lawyers frequently assume direction of estate administration, largely because most people are intimidated by probate and believe that only a lawyer can handle the tasks involved.

What such people don't recognize is that, even when a lawyer assumes responsibility for estate administration, the personal representative often does most of the work involved in gathering information about the estate. The lawyer then simply fills in a few forms, files the papers and makes brief appearances at the required court hearings, if any. For performing these tasks, a lawyer can collect several thousand dollars from the estate, money that more appropriately should go to the heirs.

A second option that is advantageous for most estates is to complete most of the work yourself and retain a lawyer on an hourly basis for occasional consultation. With this arrangement, you can collect all the relevant information about the estate, file all the required forms, compute and pay taxes and disburse the assets. When you have a question, need help or want to have your paperwork reviewed for technical accuracy, you can consult the lawyer and pay by the hour.

It is always worth trying to hire a lawyer by the hour. It lets you complete much of the work yourself and seek legal advice only when you need it. Usually, the lawyer's time in such an arrangement amounts to only a few hours. For example, a personal representative in Maryland hired a lawyer to help probate his mother's $112,000 estate. The lawyer agreed to an hourly rate of $75 and spent less than three hours advising the personal representative (mostly by telephone) on forms, filings and taxes. The legal bill for probating the estate was $210. If a lawyer had been hired under Maryland's customary percentage arrangement, the legal fee could have been nearly $6,000!

For more information about hiring a lawyer and negotiating attorney fee contracts, read HALT's *Citizens Legal Manual,* **Using a Lawyer.**

Personal Representatives' Fees

The personal representative of an estate, whether named in the will or appointed by the court, is often the surviving spouse of the deceased or a close friend or relative. Normally, such a personal representative will receive some inheritance from the estate. It is customary in such cases to waive a commission. When a family member or friend serving as personal representative does claim a commission, it seldom results in overcharging or problems among the heirs.

Be aware, however, that it is not uncommon for the lawyer who drafted the will to be named in it as personal representative. This *does not mean* the fees for the estate lawyer and personal repesentative have to be combined, but in some states, it is legally permissible for a lawyer acting as personal representative to charge the estate the *combined maximum* for *both* commissions.

Banks and trust companies are also frequently named to act as personal representative for estates. They can be named by the will, by the heirs or by the court if there is no will. A bank's estate and trust department or a trust company can provide valuable services to complex estates. If an estate is large, and if no relatives or friends are able to administer its assets, then such a corporate personal representative offers the security of responsible and experienced management. Also, if an estate has assets invested in volatile markets (*e.g.,* stocks or commodities), banks and trust companies can efficiently manage or reinvest the assets while the estate is being probated. Corporate representatives can also be counted on not to move to another location, die or otherwise be unavailable to perform the necessary duties.

The benefits of corporate personal representatives must be weighed, however, against the cost of their services and the likelihood that a non-professional can do the same tasks at little or no cost. As explained throughout this manual, probate for most estates consists mostly of routine paperwork. Research has shown that for such "paper-shuffling," banks acting as personal representative in one state charged fees averaging $7,023.

Banks and trust companies also tend to engage lawyers, often from the firm of one of the bank's or company's directors, to "ensure" the technical accuracy of their estate work. These lawyers are hired — and paid by the estate — even though the officers of banks and trust companies are thoroughly familiar with their state's probate laws and taxes, and routinely probate estates.

Appeal of Fees

Most states allow any interested person to petition the probate court for a reduction of the fees requested by the lawyer or the personal representative. Objections to fees must be filed with the court within one or two months of the notice of closing and the release of the final accounting.

It is difficult to prove that fees for probate work are unreasonable when the customary practice is to award a percentage of an estate's value and when the statutory language defining what is "reasonable" is unclear. It is even more difficult if you do not have proof of the amount of time and effort spent on the estate by the lawyer or personal representative.

One strategy is to divide a fee request by the lawyer's usual hourly rate and point out how much time the lawyer's services supposedly required. If you know that administering the estate consisted mostly of a few simple clerical tasks and shouldn't have taken more than a few hours, call the court's attention to this. The probate registrar will explain the requirements for your petition to reduce fees.

After you have filed a petition to reduce the fee requests of the personal representative or lawyer, he or she will probably respond with evidence or testimony showing that the fees are customary — and therefore "reasonable" — under the circumstances. The court will then review the matter and make its decision.

Until the court rules on the petition, the closing of the estate and distribution of assets cannot go forward. Unfortunately, probate courts rarely grant a reduction in probate fee requests. Don't let this deter you from asking that excessive fees be reduced, however, because you do have *some* chance of success.

Chapter 11
CLOSING THE ESTATE

Once you have collected the estate's assets, filed the inventory and appraisal with the court, paid all valid claims and expenses and completed the tax returns, you are ready to close the estate. Once that is done, you can distribute the assets to the heirs.

The time it takes to complete the probate of an estate can vary from a few months to two years or more, but most estates are closed and distributed within 18 months. The delay is caused by the required waiting periods for notices and for processing final accounts and tax returns. When the process is court-supervised, the personal representative can ask the court to close the estate anytime after the waiting period for submitting claims. When it is unsupervised, closing usually means merely distributing all the assets to the heirs after the creditors have been paid.

The Final Account

To close the estate, prepare a final accounting and either file it with the court or give it to the heirs, depending on whether the administration is supervised or unsupervised. The final account is a balance sheet that displays the total assets and expenses, including taxes.

The assets include everything listed on the initial inventory plus any assets discovered or received during administration. The expenses include everything the deceased person owed at the time of death, fees for the personal representative and other professional fees and expenses resulting from a last illness, the funeral, court costs, etc.

To get the balance of the estate, subtract the expenses from the assets. Calculate the state inheritance tax and other taxes due on the balance, minus all applicable exemptions. Finally, show on the balance sheet or closing form both the taxes and the planned distribution of the remainder of the estate — that is, show who will get what.

Closing Supervised Estates

When probate is court-supervised, you must file the final account with the probate registrar, along with all relevant cancelled checks and receipts. This will prove your expenses and confirm the distribution of assets already disbursed. The registrar may then conduct an "audit" of the final account. Don't be alarmed by this term. It only means the registrar will check your arithmetic.

Closing by Sworn Statement

After the audit, the estate may be closed officially either by sworn statement or by petition for court settlement. Closing by sworn statement is simple. You submit a completed form to the registrar swearing that you have properly published all required notices, paid all valid claims and the expenses of administration, filed all required tax returns and either have paid the taxes or have the appropriate consent-to-transfer-property forms, and that you have distributed or will distribute all of the estate's remaining assets to the persons legally entitled to receive them. If you use this procedure, remember that a copy of the final account and of the sworn statement must be sent to all interested persons.

The probate registrar can help you with any other questions about local procedures for closing by sworn statement. If no interested persons or creditors object to the court within one year after you file the closing statement, your responsibilities as personal representative are officially ended.

Closing by Court Petition

Some states require you to close the estate by petitioning the probate court for a *court settlement*. This is more time-consuming and troublesome, but for most estates it is no more complicated. The difference between closing by sworn statement and closing by petition is that the latter requires a final probate court hearing.

You can petition the court for a judicial settlement anytime after the waiting period for submitting claims has expired. A final accounting must be submitted to the court with the petition. Any interested person may ask for a judicial settlement, but only after a specified time has elapsed since the appointment of a personal representative.

When the petition has been received and reviewed by the court, a hearing date is set. The petitioner must give advance notice of the final hearing to all interested persons and creditors of the estate.

The final hearing usually lasts less than 10 minutes. At this hearing, the court can resolve questions raised by the personal representative, creditors or other interested persons. For example, the court may resolve a will contest; rule on the fees requested by the personal representative or attorney; waive tax liens to allow the transfer of property, or simply approve the final accounting and distribution of the estate. At the hearing, the court then issues a decree ordering the final distribution of assets.

After the hearing, or after you file for closing, you will receive a final bill for registrar's fees, court costs and unpaid taxes. This will be accompanied or followed upon payment by formal notification that you can close the estate and distribute the assets to the heirs.

Chapter 12

DISTRIBUTING THE ASSETS

In distributing the estate's assets, you must obey the deceased person's will or, if no valid will is found, state intestacy laws. Also, in some states the personal representative is not allowed to distribute the assets until a specified time after mailing the final account and notice of closing to all interested persons. This is intended to accommodate any last-minute objections. In most closings, however, the personal representative's discretion is relied upon in the timing of distribution.

Testate Distribution

You may need a large amount of cash to fulfill bequests left by the will, to divide the assets proportionally, or to pay debts. To raise this cash, you may have to sell some assets. If you do, you should offer it for sale and accept bids to get the best possible price. However, first discuss the sale of property with the principal heirs, as they may object or suggest alternative arrangements. Remember, too, that the sale of an estate's real property is sometimes restricted. (See "Real Estate Sales," Chapter 7.)

On the other hand, handle carefully any buying of estate property by the personal representative or by any relatives or associates of the personal representative. If you contemplate such a purchase, you should consult with the probate registrar or an attorney about possible conflicts of interest that might void the sale if any interested person objects.

'Distribution in Kind'

Rather than force the sale of assets (because it is complicated, because probate sales do not always bring the best price or because it may inflate the value of the estate when it comes to calculating fees), the probate codes of most states encourage *distribution in kind*. This means that if an heir stands to inherit cash under the will or by a proportional division of the estate, the physical assets of the estate may be distributed in place of their cash value.

Property distributed in kind should be valued as of the date it is distributed, not the date of death. Distribution in kind may take place in any state that allows it *unless*: (1) the heirs demand cash; (2) the current market value of the property doesn't equal the cash that is due, or (3) an heir entitled to the property as part of the *residuary estate* asks that it remain in the estate.

The Residuary Estate

The *residuary estate* is what is left after all bequests or grants have been made to heirs named in the will. The balance (*residue*) is then distributed according to the *residuary clause* of the will. This must be distributed "in kind" unless it is necessary to divide the assets between heirs. If it is left to two or more heirs, a "date of distribution" value must be calculated to assure a fair and accurate division.

Some estates lack enough assets to cover all of the distributions called for in the will. In such instances, some heirs may have their share in the estate *abated*. That is, they will lose part or all of their share. The law provides that when this is required, certain heirs must be excluded before others. If you are faced with this situation, consult with the probate registrar or an attorney.

Intestate Distribution

When no valid will can be found, you must distribute the assets according to the laws of intestacy in the state where the decedent legally resided. The *heirs-at-law* (heirs determined by law when there is no will) and their respective shares of the estate are specified in each state's intestacy laws. The personal representative simply follows the directions of these intestacy statutes. (See Appendix I and ask the probate registrar for further details.)

Distribution to Minors

Assets intended for heirs who are minors, mentally incompetent or otherwise under some form of guardianship usually must be given to their guardians in trust for their care, but relatively small sums — usually $5,000 or less — may be distributed to parents instead of a court-appointed guardian if the state has enacted the Uniform Probate Code (UPC). In some non-UPC states, small sums of money or other assets may also be distributed to the parents of a minor child without the appointment of a guardian, if the court approves.

In UPC states it is common to invest a minor's share of an estate in an insured savings account, in savings certificates or in bonds, sometimes deposited with the court until the minor reaches the age of majority (18 or 21, depending on the state). For information about the distribution of intestate estate assets to minors and about the appointment of guardians, see the section on "Appointment of Guardians" in Chapter 2.

Distribution Records

When you distribute the assets among the heirs (distributees), be sure to get a receipt from each one acknowledging that he or she received his or her full share of the estate. In some states, you may have to deposit these receipts with the court before you will be discharged from your responsibilities as personal representative. In other states, you will automatically be discharged after a certain time if no one objects to the distribution of assets or to the way you administered the estate.

In either case, for a few years after the estate is closed, you should keep in a safe place copies of all receipts for distribution and payment of claims. Your records will help protect you from liability in the unlikely event that questions arise later on.

Under the Uniform Probate Code, any assets that are improperly distributed may be recovered and redistributed up to one year after the date of distribution or three years after the person died, whichever is later. This law protects rightful heirs from mistakes that go unnoticed when the estate is closed.

This concludes the probate process. The next chapter, "Small-Estate Administration," describes procedures that may be followed in some states for estates with few assets. Following the concluding chapter of the manual, you will find a "Personal Representative Checklist." This will help you remember to complete all tasks required of the personal representative. Appendix I immediately following the checklist provides specific information about probate rules in all 50 states, Puerto Rico, the Virgin Islands and the District of Columbia.

Chapter 13

SMALL-ESTATE ADMINISTRATION

If the nature and value of an estate's property that is subject to probate meet state requirements, the process may require only a few simple steps. This shortened process is called *small-estate administration,* sometimes referred to as *summary administration* or *administration unnecessary.* Even some relatively large estates can qualify, so be sure to look into the eligibility requirements.

Most states require similar basic steps. Some merely require a simple *affidavit* (a sworn statement) attesting to the death and the names of the heirs. Others require a court order for the transfer of assets. And still others require an inventory and appraisal of estate assets and notice of administration to all heirs and creditors.

Conditions for Summary Administration

Estates qualify for small-estate administration only if certain conditions are met. The states generally require that the probate estate's value not exceed a maximum amount and not include any *solely-owned real property* (land or buildings).

The maximum dollar-value eligible for small-estate administration ranges between $10,000 and $20,000 in most states. These figures are a little misleading, however. When valuing the estate to determine its eligibility, you can exclude certain large assets that are part of the *gross estate* (the total of all assets, whether subject to probate or not.)

The dollar limits apply only to the deceased person's *solely-owned probate assets,* such as vehicles, stocks, bonds and bank accounts registered only in the decedent's name. Assets held in joint ownership or in trust can probably be excluded when calculating the value of the probate estate. The same is true for insurance benefits that name a beneficiary.

Some states allow you also to deduct the value of vehicles, along with the value of any liens or encumbrances on the property that is subject to probate. The value of homestead exemptions and family allowances as defined in state law also may be excluded. The states that recognize *community property* allow half of the value of the community property to be deducted from the probate estate when one spouse dies. Some states allow still other deductions. For more information about non-probate assets that can be deducted from the estate's value in determining whether or not it is eligible for small-estate administration, see Chapter 8 and ask the probate registrar.

Because of all the available deductions, even a relatively large estate that includes both personal and real property may qualify for small-estate administration. For example, the gross estate may be worth $50,000, but if it includes a $40,000 home held in joint tenancy with the spouse, the probate estate is worth only $10,000. In a state that defines small estates as those worth no more than $10,000, the estate would qualify.

Appointment of Claimant

In small-estate administration, the person handling the estate is often called the "claimant" rather than personal repesentative. Whether or not you may serve as claimant in small-estate administration may also depend upon your relation to the deceased, because some states allow only the surviving spouse or children to use the abbreviated procedures.

Other states allow any heirs to use small-estate procedures, regardless of their relationship to the decedent. In these states, the only significantly different requirements are that, usually, the person distributing the estate must be bonded, that interested persons must be notified that small-estate administration procedures are being used, and that the person handling the estate remain subject to claims by creditors and interested persons longer than would be necessary for a member of the immediate family.

Using small- estate procedures is actually easier than determining whether you and the estate qualify to use them. The two types of small-estate administration are *summary* and *administration unnecessary*. "Summary administration" uses streamlined procedures that usually require you to give notice of administration to all interested persons and file an inventory of the assets with the court. "Administration unnecessary" means that probate administration is not required at all. In states that allow it, it is reserved for only the smallest estates.

Transferring property under both summary administration and administration unnecessary is accomplished in one of two ways, by affidavit or by judicial order.

Transfer by Affidavit

In most states a simple "do-it-yourself" affidavit is all that's needed to transfer property. Affidavit forms are available at the probate court and at legal stationery stores. To collect or transfer the assets by affidavit, you need only complete and sign the form and, probably, file a copy with the registrar.

You must sign the form in front of a notary public and then present it to each person from whom property is to be collected or to each official responsible for transferring title to the property. An original notarized affidavit form must be presented *for each item of property*. A certified copy of the death certificate, evidence that the property was solely-owned by the decedent and proof that you are legally entitled to it may also be required.

If property is to be divided between two or more heirs, each one must complete and present a notarized affidavit. Nominal service fees may also have to be paid.

Transfer by Judicial Order

In states with more formal small-estate procedures, a few additional steps are required. You may have to file a full inventory and appraisal of the estate's assets with the court, along with a certified copy of the death certificate, proof that you are legally entitled to receive the property and a petition for a small-estate proceeding. If the court grants your petition, the judge will issue a written order you can use to obtain the release or transfer of title to the assets.

In effect, the judge's order replaces the "do-it-yourself" affidavit with formal court instructions. Once you have the order, the procedure is the same: you must present a certified order from the judge for each item of property to anyone holding estate property or responsible for transferring its title. In some states you may also be required to post bond and serve notice of small-estate administration to all interested persons and creditors.

Collecting the Property

Upon presentation of either the affidavit or a court order, any person holding estate property must promptly release it or transfer its title to you. Your affidavit and the petition to the court for small-estate administration are both executed under penalty of perjury, and anyone who releases property to you is fully protected by law from liability when that release is based on a properly executed affidavit or court order.

Collecting or transferring property located outside the state where the deceased person resided may be more difficult. You may have to go there with an affidavit or court order in hand. Alternatively, you can appoint a resident of the state in which the property is located to collect it or effect its transfer. See the section on "Ancillary Administration" in Chapter 4 and check with your probate registrar or a bank for further details.

Taxes and Exemptions

If estate or inheritance taxes are due on a small estate, you may have to pay the taxes or get a *consent-to-transfer* or *release-of-inheritance-tax-lien* form from the state tax authorities before claiming property. Generally, however, the surviving spouse, children and grandchildren will not have to pay taxes on property that is eligible for small-estate administration.

Other heirs using small estate procedures may be responsible for taxes and should inquire about them with the probate registrar or state tax authorities.

Some states protect the home of the surviving spouse and minor children with homestead laws or exemptions. These protect the home from the claims of creditors and interested persons. They apply *even if the will disinherited these survivors*. For more information see Chapter 7.

Disputes over property transferred or subject to transfer under small-estate administration can be resolved by the probate court, but such disputes are rare. The transfer of small-estate assets under summary administration or administration-unnecessary procedures, whether by "do-it-yourself" affidavit or by court order, is uncomplicated and nearly automatic. Probate court personnel can help you determine if the estate qualifies for these procedures and help you complete the required forms. Usually, nothing else is needed.

CONCLUSION

For most estates, probate could and should be a simple matter. Typically, it consists of appraising the estate's assets, filing standard forms, paying taxes, settling claims against the estate and distributing what's left among the heirs.

Unfortunately, the essential simplicity has been hidden from the average American. The diversity of state probate codes, the unnecessarily complex language, forms and procedures in many states, and the economic interests of the various professions involved in probate administration have combined to make the tasks involved appear more complex than they are.

Some of the apparent complexity results from archaic laws desperately in need of revision, but more often than not, the aura of complexity that surrounds probate is a deliberate smokescreen used by lawyers and others to justify hourly fees of $1,000 or more.

Probate Reform Efforts

Two probate reform movements seek to eliminate the unnecessary cost and complexity. One effort, led by the National Conference of Commissioners on Uniform State Laws, is an attempt to have the Uniform Probate Code (UPC) enacted in all states. The second, led by HALT, seeks to reduce immediately the costs of probate through legislative measures that would allow the use of more "self-help" procedures and materials.

The UPC simplifies many probate procedures and eliminates direct court supervision of estate administration, thus giving the personal representative freedom to conduct probate independently and reducing both delays and costs.

HALT supports legislation that simplifies probate, specifically outlaws percentage fees for probate work, or requires itemized justification of "reasonable fees" based on hourly rates. To reduce further the dependence of citizens on expensive professionals, HALT also supports measures to require "over-the-counter" assistance on routine probate matters from court personnel, the development of instructional materials and increased competition among competent non-professionals for probate-related services.

The Citizens Legal Manual

The reform measures discussed above will require considerable grassroots support to be adopted by most state legislatures. Building such support is a time-consuming process, but it is vitally necessary. Until effective reforms are passed in every state, citizens will have to cut through the legal jargon and overcome the resistance of the probate industry on their own initiative.

This manual is intended to help citizens do just that by lifting the veil of mystery that obscures the probate process. If consumers demonstrate that they can conduct probate in spite of the present costs and complexity, the arguments for implementing self-help probate procedures will be even more compelling. For more information about HALT and its program for legal reform, see the last page of this manual.

P. R. CHECKLIST

This checklist will help you remember the probate tasks you may have to perform as personal representative. Not everything listed will be necessary for every estate, but each item should be reviewed to determine whether it applies to the estate you are administering.

The list follows the general order of probate tasks, but it is not meant to be followed rigidly. Your state's probate rules and the estate you are administering may require some variation in the order of events. Each item in the list is followed by a number. This number refers to the chapter or chapters of this manual where the topic is discussed.

___ Locate the last will of the decedent (2)

___ Submit the will to the court to be "proved" (2)

___ Obtain notarized affidavits from the will's witnesses, if necessary (2)

___ Consider surviving spouse's right of election (2)

___ If there is no will, submit an intestacy form to the court (2)

___ Apply for appointment as P.R. (3)

___ Post bond, if required (3)

___ Notify all interested persons of the opening of probate (3)

___ Arrange publication of notice to creditors (3, 6)

___ Notify post office, utilities, credit companies, etc. of decedent's death (2, 3)

___ Obtain letters of administration (3)

___ If possible, choose between supervised, unsupervised and small-estate administration (4, 13)

___ Examine financial records and recent tax returns of the deceased (5)

___ Inventory all safe deposit boxes (2)

___ Prepare preliminary estimate of estate's value (5)

___ Open estate bank accounts (5)

___ Appraise the assets for "date of death" value (5)

___ Hire professional appraisers, if court requires (5)

___ Apply for state and, if necessary, federal tax identification numbers (5, 9)

___ Collect all property of or owed to the estate (5)

___ Inspect all real estate and examine mortgages, leases, etc. (7)

___ Arrange for ancillary administration of property in other states (4)

___ Arrange for the management of special concerns (e.g., stock investments) (10)

___ Identify all non-probate property (e.g., trusts and jointly-owned property) (8)

___ Examine non-probate property for tax consequences to estate (8)

___ Deliver all trust property to trustees (8)

___ Check with decedent's employer for unpaid salary and employee benefits (8)

___ File for any social security, civil service and veterans' benefits (8)

___ File claims for life insurance and other insurance benefits (8)

___ Examine insurance policies and make adjustments if necessary (8)

___ Prepare a detailed inventory and appraisal of the entire estate (5)

___ File the inventory with court or heirs (5)

___ File the decedent's personal income tax returns (state and federal) (9)

___ File state inheritance or estate tax returns (9)

___ File tax returns for property in other states (9)

___ File estate income tax returns (state and federal) for period of administration (9)

___ File federal estate tax return within nine months, if necessary (9)

___ Obtain "consent to transfer" forms from the tax authorities (9)

___ Check at the court for claims filed against the estate (6)

___ Determine the cash needs of the estate (12)

___ Arrange sale of estate property, if necessary (7, 12)

___ Pay all valid claims, bills and expenses (with court approval, if required) (6, 12)

___ Petition court for personal representative's and attorney's fees, if any (10)

___ Prepare final account of estate assets and their distribution (11)

___ File final account with the court, if necessary (11)

___ Close the estate (11)

___ List specific distributions indicated in the will (12)

___ Discuss "distribution in kind" arrangements with heirs (12)

___ Consider division of residuary estate (12)

___ Consider necessity of appointing guardians for minors (2, 12)

___ Distribute all assets (with court clearance, if required) (12)

___ Obtain receipts for all assets distributed (12)

___ Obtain discharge of personal representative from the court, if required (12)

___ File copies of all records in a personal file for at least two years (12)

Appendix I
STATE RULES

This appendix gives essential rules for probate in all 50 states, the District of Columbia, Puerto Rico and the Virgin Islands. The information incorporates changes in probate laws through 1985 or 1986, depending on the state. The year of the latest amendments included in the research is noted for each state under **Statutes**. Laws and court rules may change at any time, however, so before proceeding, check your state's probate code (see *Dealing With the Probate Code* in the **Introduction** to this manual) or ask the probate clerk.

When a state code uses terms that are different from those commonly used in this manual, those terms are included in parentheses. The following notes should help you understand the entries in this appendix. Other categories and headings are self-explanatory. (Throughout the appendix, the abbreviation "P.R." stands for Personal Representative.)

Administration

Unsupervised refers to an informal probate procedure that requires little or no supervision. *Supervised* refers to a formal procedure that requires court approval at major procedural steps. If hearings and notice are required before each step, it is usually called *Formal*. If not, it is usually called *Informal*.

Summary and *Administration Unnecessary* generally apply to small estates for which a streamlined procedure can be used. *By Affidavit* refers to a procedure for small estates by which an inheritor can collect certain property simply by signing an affidavit. See Chapters 4 and 13 for further discussion of administration procedures.

Spouse's Automatic Share

Almost every state allows a spouse to receive some property automatically when the other spouse dies. This usually includes household goods and the right to remain in the house and protect it against creditors, plus living expenses during administration or longer. Check your code or ask the probate clerk whether and how to apply to the court for this "automatic" share. Do not confuse it with either the *Spouse's Intestate Share* or the *Spouse's Right of Election*, both discussed below.

Spouse's Intestate Share

Each state divides differently the property of someone who dies without a will (*intestate*). This entry explains the spouse's share. Keep in mind that other relatives will divide the balance of the estate according to your state's laws. Check your probate code.

Entire estate refers to the transfer of all of the deceased person's property to the spouse. When the spouse receives less than the entire estate, it is critical to know how your state decides what assets are included in the estate. For example, in most UPC states, the total value of the estate is calculated to include the surviving spouse's share of property owned jointly by both spouses but not funeral or last-illness costs. Although some of this information is included in this appendix, if you are in doubt about what is included in your estate, check the probate code or ask the probate clerk.

Separate property is all property acquired by either spouse before marriage or as a gift or inheritance during marriage. Most other property acquired during marriage, like salaries, is ***community property***.

The term *issue* refers to children, grandchildren, great-grandchildren, etc. All terms refer to blood relationships. Most states, however, allow adopted children to inherit property the same as natural children do.

Spouse's Right of Election

Most states protect husbands and wives from being disinherited by giving them a ***Right of Election Against the Will***. However, the share that a spouse may elect under this provision is generally less than the share offered under intestacy laws.

A decision to "elect against the will" almost always means that the spouse forfeits any right to a share assigned in the will. After such an election, the balance of the estate is divided among the remaining beneficiaries according to the state's intestacy law.

Proving Will

Formal and informal proof of will should not be confused with formal and informal ***administration***. The terms refer to the requirements for proof. For example, a will may require formal proof even in the informal procedure of unsupervised administration.

A ***self-proved*** will is generally considered valid or "proved" if it was properly executed and notarized. (See *Proving the Will*, Chapter 2.)

Notice

This entry explains when and how notification must be given. Some states combine the requirements by considering publication of a notice to creditors as sufficient notice to heirs and others interested in the estate. These are identified in the appendix.

Typically, the required notices include informing all those who could take by intestacy or the will that you are applying for appointment as P.R., that the estate is being opened to prove the will and that you have been appointed P.R. Such notices also include notification of the deadlines for making claims against the estate.

Notices To Creditors usually involve publishing a notice in a newspaper informing creditors about the death, your appointment as P.R. and the deadline for filing claims. Check with your court clerk or probate code to see whether your state also requires notices of the inventory or that the estate is being closed.

ALABAMA: Probate Court
Statutes: Code of Alabama 1975 (Amendments to 1985), Title 43.
Administration: *Supervised* — For all estates except as follows. *Summary* — For estates with only personal property less than $3,000 after debts if closest living relative applies.
Spouse's Automatic Share: Homestead up to $6,000, personal property up to $3,500 and family expenses during administration; if estate insolvent, family expenses up to 1 year.
Spouse's Intestate Share: 1) Entire estate if no living issue or parent; 2) $50,000 plus 1/2 balance if living parent but no living issue or living issue are all surviving spouse's; 3) 1/2 estate if 1 or more living issue are not surviving spouse's.
Spouse's Right of Election: Lesser of — 1) 1/3 estate or 2) entire estate minus spouse's separate estate. Must elect within 6 months of death or 6 months of proving the will, whichever is later.
Proving Will: Testimony of 1 signing witness; if unavailable, by 1 witness proving handwriting of deceased and of 1 signing witness. Self-proved wills accepted.
Nonresident P.R.: Yes, if named in will.
Notice: *Before Proving Will* — At least 10 days before hearing, give (in-state) or mail (out-of-state) to spouse and those who could take by intestacy or will. Instead, court may allow notice to be published once a week for 3 consecutive weeks before hearing. *Before Summary Hearing* — Upon petition for hearing, publish once a week for 3 consecutive weeks; if no local newspaper, post in courthouse 3 consecutive weeks. *After P.R. Appointment, to Creditors* — Within 1 month of appointment, publish once a week for 3 consecutive weeks.
Forms of Property: Tenancy in common presumed for real estate held jointly with no express right of survivorship. No tenancy by entirety.
Inventory, Appraisal: Within 2 months of appointment P.R. may hire private appraiser.
Claims: Within 6 months of appointment.
P.R. Fees: Up to 2.5% of all income, payments of debts and personal property.
Attorney Fees: Set by court. Fee for sale of real estate in will limited to $100.
Note: Laws differ in each county. In many counties, judges receive commissions based on work done. In Jefferson and Mobile counties, judges also have power to fashion a "fair" settlement.

ALASKA: Superior Court
Statutes: Alaska Statutes 1962 (Amendments to 1985), Title 13 (UPC).

Appendix I

Administration: *Unsupervised (Independent)* — For all estates except as follows. *Supervised* — Upon petition, court imposes limited or complete supervision ranging from stopping a sale to continuing control of estate. *Summary* — If estate (minus some real estate claims) totals less than spouse's exemptions plus administration, funeral and last-illness costs. *By Affidavit* — Collect personal property if estate (minus some real estate claims) is less than $15,000, if inheritor applies at least 30 days after death and no P.R. application is pending.

Spouse's Automatic Share: Homestead up to $27,000, personal property up to $10,000 and "reasonable" family expenses for 1 year.

Spouse's Intestate Share: 1) Entire estate if no living issue or parent; 2) $50,000 plus 1/2 balance if living parent but no living issue, or living issue are all surviving spouse's; 3) 1/2 estate if 1 or more living issue are not surviving spouse's.

Spouse's Right of Election: 1/3 estate including property transferred to spouse in which the deceased retained an interest. Must elect within 9 months of death or 6 months after proving will, whichever is later.

Proving Will: *Informal Hearing* — Testimony or affidavit of anyone with knowledge of execution. *Formal Hearing [Uncontested]* — Testimony or affidavit of 1 signing witness; if unavailable, other evidence. *[Contested]* — Testimony of 1 signing witness; if witnesses out-of-state or insane, other evidence. Self-proved wills accepted.

Nonresident P.R.: Yes.

Notice: *Before Proving Will [Formal Hearing]* — At least 14 days before hearing, mail to spouse, P.R. and those who could take by intestacy or will; if address unknown, publish once a week for 3 weeks, the last time at least 10 days before hearing. *[Informal Hearing]* — Same as above except only to P.R. or upon request. *After Proving Will [Formal Hearing]* — None required. *[Informal Hearing]* — Within 30 days, mail to those who could take by intestacy or will whose addresses are available. *Before P.R. Appointment [Informal Hearing]* — Same as Before Proving Will, except only to those with same or greater right to be P.R. or upon request. *[Formal Hearing]* — Same as for Informal Hearing. *After P.R. Appointment, to Creditors* — If notice not already given, publish once a week for 3 consecutive weeks. *Summary Administration* — None required.

Forms of Property: No joint tenancy in personal property. Persons with undivided interests in real estate are tenants in common. Spouses hold real estate as tenants by entirety unless stated otherwise.

Inventory, Appraisal: Within 3 months of appointment or upon request. Court-appointed appraiser must assess all non-

cash assets; P.R. may assess when cash value equals face value.
Claims: Within 4 months of first published notice. If no notice, within 3 years of death.
P.R. Fees: Reasonable fee (usually no court supervision).
Attorney Fees: Reasonable fee (usually no court supervison).

ARIZONA: Superior Court
Statutes: Arizona Revised Statutes 1975 (Amendments to 1985), Title 14 (UPC).
Administration: *Unsupervised (Independent)* — For all estates except as follows. *Supervised* — Upon petition, court imposes limited or complete supervision ranging from stopping a sale to continuing control of estate. *Summary* — If estate (minus some real estate claims) totals less than allowances and exempt property plus administration, funeral and last-illness costs. *By Affidavit* — Collect real estate if estate (minus some claims) is less than $15,000, inheritor applies at least 6 months after death, no P.R. application pending and all costs paid for last illness, funeral, unsecured debts and taxes; collect personal property and payment for debts if estate's personal property is less than $30,000, inheritor applies at least 30 days after death and no P.R. application pending; collect vehicles and earnings owed deceased up to $5,000 if inheritor applies.
Spouse's Automatic Share: 1/2 community property, homestead up to $6,000, personal property up to $3,500 and reasonable family expenses during administration; if estate insolvent, family expenses up to 1 year.
Spouse's Intestate Share: 1) Entire estate if no living issue or if all living issue are also surviving spouse's; 2) 1/2 separate property but none of 1/2 community property of deceased if 1 or more living issue are not surviving spouse's.
Spouse's Right of Election: No provision.
Proving Will: *Informal Hearing* — Testimony or affidavit of anyone with knowledge of execution. *Formal Hearing* *[Uncontested]* — Testimony or affidavit of 1 signing witness. *[Contested]* — Testimony of 1 signing witness; if unavailable, other evidence. Self-proved wills accepted.
Nonresident P.R.: Yes.
Notice: *Before Proving Will [Formal Hearing]* — At least 14 days before hearing mail to spouse, P.R. and those who could take by intestacy or will; if address unknown, publish 3 times with first publication 14 days before hearing. *[Informal Hearing]* — Same as for Formal Hearing above except only to P.R. or upon request. *After Proving Will [Formal Hearing]* — None required. *[Informal Hearing]* — Within 10 days give or mail to spouse and those who could take by intestacy or will if addresses

are reasonably available. **Before P.R. Appointment** *[Formal Hearing]* — Same as Before Proving Will except also send to those with same or greater right to be P.R. *[Informal Hearing]* — Same as Before Proving Will except only to those with same or greater right to be P.R. or upon request. **After P.R. Appointment** *[Formal Hearing]* — None required. *[Informal Hearing]* — Same as After Proving Will. **Summary Administration** — None required. **To Creditors** — Promptly publish once a week for 3 consecutive weeks.
Forms of Property: Community property. Property acquired during marriage outside state before moving into state is quasi-community property controlled by Arizona law. Joint tenancy between spouses if stated. No tenancy by entirety.
Inventory, Appraisal: Within 3 months of appointment. P.R. may hire private appraiser.
Claims: Within 4 months of first creditor notice.
P.R. Fees: Reasonable fee.
Attorney Fees: Reasonable fee.

ARKANSAS: Probate Court
Statutes: Arkansas Statutes Annotated 1949 (Amendments to 1985), Titles 60-63.
Administration: *Supervised* — For all estates except as follows. *Administration Unnecessary* — For solvent estates of less than $25,000 after debts and spouse's exemptions if no P.R. application is pending and at least 45 days after death.
Spouse's Automatic Share: Homestead up to $2,500, personal property up to $1,000 before creditors or $2,000 before others, furnishings reasonably necessary for family, family expenses up to $500 per month for time set by court and lifetime oil/gas rights.
Spouse's Intestate Share: 1) Entire estate if married to deceased more than 3 years and no living issue; 2) 1/2 of estate if married to deceased less than 3 years and no living issue; 3) nothing if living issue.
Spouse's Right of Election: 1) 1/3 real estate owned by deceased during marriage and 1/3 personal property owned at death if married to deceased more than 1 year and has surviving child; 2) 1/2 estate before heirs or 1/3 before creditors if no surviving child; 3) lifetime use of 1/2 real estate before heirs or 1/3 before creditors and 1/2 personal property if real estate has been owned by the family at least two generations. Must elect within 1 month of deadline for filing claims unless spouse's share is uncertain, then 1 month after litigation regarding share ends.
Proving Will: Testimony of 2 signing witnesses; if out of U.S. or insane, by testimony of 2 witnesses proving handwriting of

deceased and of unavailable signing witness. Self-proved wills accepted.
Nonresident P.R.: Yes, if named in will and appoint local agent.
Notice: *Before Proving Will [Uncontested]* — Not required. *[Contested]* — Give (at least 10 days before hearing) or mail (at least 15 days before hearing) to those who could take by intestacy or will or (at least 15 days before hearing) publish once a week for 2 consecutive weeks and mail to those named on application for probate. *After P.R. Appointment* — Within 1 month of first creditor publication, give or mail to those who could take by intestacy or will. If estate, after homestead, is less than $1,000, only post in courthouse 3 consecutive weeks. *To Creditors* — Promptly publish once a week for 2 consecutive weeks.
Forms of Property: Tenancy by entirety recognized for personal property, corporate stock, bank and savings accounts. Ownership by husband and wife creates presumption of tenancy by entirety with right of survivorship. Tenancy in common and joint tenancy also recognized.
Inventory, Appraisal: Within 2 months of appointment unless waived by those named in will. P.R. may hire private appraiser.
Claims: Within 3 months of first creditor notice; if no creditor notice, within 5 years of death.
P.R. Fees: Up to 10% of first $1,000 of personal property, 5% of next $4,000, 3% of balance. Court may allow reasonable fee for services involving real estate.
Attorney Fees: Up to 5% of first $5,000 of real estate and personal property, 4% of next $20,000, 3% of next $75,000, 2.75% of next $300,000, 2.5% of next $600,000, 2% of balance. Court may award higher fee.

CALIFORNIA: Superior Court (Probate Division)
Statutes: West's Annotated California Code, Probate Code 1956 (Amendments to 1985), Vols. 52-54, Sec. 1-1700.
Administration: *Unsupervised (Independent)* — For all estates except as follows. *Summary* — For estates (minus real estate gifts to surviving spouse, life insurance, vehicles and salary up to $5,000) less than $60,000 including less than $10,000 California real estate if a close relative applies. *Non-Probate Transfer* — Spouse collects all property left by will or intestacy.
Spouse's Automatic Share: 1/2 community property and intestate share unless spouse signed written waiver, was clearly omitted from will or provided for by property transfers, plus use of home until 60 days after filing inventory; longer at court's discretion.

Appendix I

Spouse's Intestate Share: 1/2 quasi-community property (property acquired during marriage when California was not couple's permanent home state), plus 1) 1/2 separate property if child or issue of 1 deceased child or if no issue except parents and/or their issue; 2) 1/3 separate property if 1 child or 1 child and issue of 1 deceased child or issue of 2 deceased children; 3) otherwise, all separate property.
Spouse's Right of Election: No provision.
Proving Will: Testimony of 1 signing witness; if unavailable, by affidavit; if unavailable for affidavit, testimony or affidavit of anyone with knowledge of will's execution or deceased person's handwriting. Self-proved wills accepted.
Nonresident P.R.: Yes.
Notice: *Before Proving Will, P.R. Appointment* — At least 10 days before hearing publish 3 times with 5 days between first and last publication and mail to spouse, children, those who could take by intestacy or will, creditors and anyone with same or greater right to be P.R.
Forms of Property: Community property. Property in names of spouses as joint tenants is not community property unless stated. Joint tenancy must be stated. No tenancy by entirety.
Inventory, Appraisal: Within 3 months of appointment. P.R. must hire appraiser for all non-cash assets; P.R. may appraise other property if actual value matches face value.
Claims: Within 4 months of appointment.
P.R. Fees: Up to 4% of first $15,000, 3% of next $85,000, 2% of next $900,000, 1% of balance plus necessary expenses.
Attorney Fees: Same as P.R.

COLORADO: District Court (Denver — Probate Court)
Statutes: Colorado Revised Statutes 1973 (Amendments to 1985), Title 15 (UPC).
Administration: *Unsupervised (Independent)* — For all estates except as follows. *Supervised* — Upon petition, court imposes limited or complete supervision ranging from stopping a sale to continuing control of estate. *Summary* — If estate (minus some real estate claims) totals less than exempt property, spouse's allowances plus administration, funeral and last-illness costs. *By Affidavit* — Collect personal property and payment for debts of estate (minus some real estate claims) less than $20,000 if 10 days have passed since death, no P.R. application pending and inheritor applies.
Spouse's Automatic Share: 1/2 community property, personal property up to $7,500 and reasonable family expenses during administration; if estate insolvent, up to 1 year.
Spouse's Intestate Share: 1) Entire estate if no living issue; 2) $25,000 plus 1/2 balance if living issue are all surviving

spouse's; 3) 1/2 estate if 1 or more living issue are not surviving spouse's.
Spouse's Right of Election: 1/2 estate. Must elect within 6 months of first creditor notice or within 1 year of death, whichever is earlier.
Proving Will: *Informal Hearing* — Testimony or affidavit of anyone with knowledge of execution. *Formal Hearing [Uncontested]* — Testimony or affidavit of 1 signing witness. *[Contested]* — Testimony of 1 signing witness; if unavailable, other evidence. Self-proved wills accepted.
Nonresident P.R.: Yes.
Notice: *Before Proving Will [Formal Hearing]* — At least 10 days before hearing, mail to spouse, P.R., those who could take by intestacy or will; if address or identity unknown, publish once a week 3 consecutive weeks with last publication 10 days before hearing. *[Informal Hearing]* — Same as above except only to P.R. and upon request. *After Proving Will [Formal Hearing]* — None required. *[Informal Hearing]* — Within 30 days, give or mail to those who could take by intestacy or will. *Before P.R. Appointment [Formal Hearing]* — Same as Before Proving Will except also send to those with same or greater right to be P.R. *[Informal Hearing]* — Same as Before Proving Will except only send to those with same or greater right to be P.R. and upon request. *After P.R. Appointment [Informal Hearing]* — If not already given, mail within 30 days. *[Formal Hearing]* — Not required. *To Creditors* — Publish once a week 3 consecutive weeks. *Summary Administration* — None required.
Forms of Property: Tenancy in common presumed unless otherwise stated. Joint tenancy recognized. No tenancy by entirety.
Inventory, Appraisal: Within 3 months of appointment. P.R. may hire private appraiser.
Claims: Within 4 months of first creditor notice or 1 year from death, whichever is earlier.
P.R. Fees: Reasonable fee.
Attorney Fees: Reasonable fee.

CONNECTICUT: Probate Court
Statutes: Connecticut General Statutes Annotated 1958 (Amendments to 1985), Title 45.
Administration: *Supervised* — For all estates except as follows. *Administration Unnecessary* — For estates after debts with only personal property less than $20,000 if closest relative applies.
Spouse's Automatic Share: Court sets living expenses.
Spouse's Intestate Share: 1) Entire estate if no living issue or parent; 2) first $100,000 plus 3/4 balance if living parent but no

living issue; 3) first $100,000 plus 1/2 balance if living issue are all surviving spouse's; 4) 1/2 estate if one or more living issue are not surviving spouse's.
Spouse's Right of Election: Lifetime use of 1/3 estate. Must elect within 2 months after all claims due.
Proving Will: No provision. Court sets at hearing. Self-proved wills accepted.
Nonresident P.R.: Yes, if named in will and grant Secretary of State power of attorney.
Notice: *Before Proving Will* — Publish, give or mail before hearing to P.R. and those who could take by intestacy or will; court determines time and method; may be waived by court if estate totals less than administration, funeral and last-illness costs, or for good cause. *After Proving Will, Before P.R. Appointment, to Creditors* — Within 10 days of court order, post on public signpost nearest where deceased last lived, publish in newspaper or other notice as court directs.
Forms of Property: In joint ownership, tenancy in common presumed unless words "joint tenants" follow names. Joint tenancy automatically includes right of survivorship. No tenancy by entirety.
Inventory, Appraisal: Within 2 months of appointment. P.R. may hire private appraiser.
Claims: Within 3-12 months of notice; set by court.
P.R. Fees: Reasonable fee.
Attorney Fees: Reasonable fee.

DELAWARE: Chancery (Register of Wills)
Statutes: Delaware Code Annotated 1974 (Amendments to 1986), Title 12.
Administration: *Supervised* — For all estates except as follows. *Administration Unnecessary* — For estates with only personal property less than $12,500 after debts, if closest relative applies, no P.R. application pending and at least 30 days passed since death.
Spouse's Automatic Share: Living expenses up to $2,000.
Spouse's Intestate Share: 1) Entire estate if no living issue or parent; 2) first $50,000 plus 1/2 balance of personal property and use of real estate during life if living parent or if living issue are all surviving spouse's; 3) 1/2 personal property plus use of real estate for life if 1 or more living issue are not surviving spouse's.
Spouse's Right of Election: Lesser of $20,000 or 1/3 adjusted gross estate as defined for federal estate taxes after lifetime transfers with surviving spouse's consent. Must elect within 6 months of P.R.'s appointment unless court grants extension.

Proving Will: Testimony of 2 signing witnesses; if unavailable, testimony and affidavit of 2 witnesses proving signatures of witnesses; if unavailable, testimony or affidavit of 2 witnesses proving signature of deceased. Self-proved wills accepted.
Nonresident P.R.: Yes, if named in will, appointed immediately; if not, after 60 days after death if no pending in-state P.R. application. Nonresident P.R. must grant Register of Wills power of attorney.
Notice: *Before Proving Will* — Upon request, provide as court directs. *After Proving Will* — Within 40 days of P.R. appointment, Register of Wills posts in county courthouse and publishes at least once a week 3 consecutive weeks.
Administration Unnecessary — None required.
Forms of Property: Tenancy in common presumed. If joint owners are married, tenancy by entirety. Joint tenancy created only if stated.
Inventory, Appraisal: Within 3 months of appointment; penalty if more than 1 month late. P.R. may hire private appraiser.
Claims: Within 6 months of appointment if notice properly given, with exceptions.
P.R., Attorney Fees: Combined P.R. and attorney fees can be up to $250 plus 11.3% of amount greater than $2,200 for estates less than $5,000; $565 plus 6.8% of amount greater than $5,000 for estates less than $10,000; $905 plus 5.6% of amount greater than $10,000 for estates less than $20,000; $1,465 plus 5.1% of amount greater than $20,000 for estates less than $30,000; $1,975 plus 4.5% of amount greater than $30,000 for estates less than $40,000; $2,425 plus 3.9% of amount greater than $40,000 for estates less than 60,000; $3,205 plus 3.7% of amount greater than $60,000 for estates less than $80,000. See Chancery Court Rules for fees on larger estates. Court can modify fee.

DISTRICT OF COLUMBIA: Superior Court (Probate Division) and Register of Wills
Statutes: District of Columbia Code Annotated 1981 (Amendments to 1985), Titles 18-20.
Administration: *Supervised* — For all estates except as follows. *Summary* — For estates less than $10,000.
Administration Unnecessary — For estates of only one or two cars.
Spouse's Automatic Share: Family expenses up to $10,000 before debts but after $750 in funeral costs.
Spouse's Intestate Share: 1) Entire estate if no living issue, parent, sibling or sibling's child; 2) 1/2 estate if living parent, sibling or sibling's child; 3) 1/3 estate if living issue.
Spouse's Right of Election: Either intestate share up to 1/2

estate after debts or lifetime use of 1/3 real estate and 1/2 other property after debts. Must elect within 6 months of proving will.
Proving Will: *Informal Hearing (Abbreviated)* — If properly executed, nothing required; if not, by affidavit of anyone with personal knowledge of execution. *Formal Hearing (Standard)* — Affidavits of witnesses. Self-proved wills accepted.
Nonresident P.R.: Yes.
Notice: *Before Proving Will [Formal Hearing]* — Upon filing petition, promptly give or mail to P.R. and those who could take by intestacy or will, plus publish once a week 2 consecutive weeks. *[Informal Hearing]* — None required. *After P.R. Appointment, to Creditors* — Within 20 days of appointment, publish once a week 3 consecutive weeks in Washington Law Reporter and local newspaper. *Summary Administration* — Only if court directs.
Forms of Property: Tenancy in common presumed unless joint tenancy stated. Joint tenancy, tenancy by entirety can be created if at least one of the granting owners is also a recipient owner. Joint ownership by husband and wife presumes tenancy by entirety.
Inventory, Appraisal: Within 3 months of appointment. Must hire court-approved appraiser for property except cash, corporate stocks sold over the counter or on exchange and debts.
Claims: Within 6 months of first creditor notice.
P.R. Fees: Reasonable fee; form must be submitted for court approval. *Summary Administration* — No fee.
Attorney Fees: Same as P.R.

FLORIDA: Circuit Court
Statutes: West's Florida Statutes Annotated 1976 (Amendments to 1986), Ch. 731-738 (Modified UPC).
Administration: *Supervised* — For all estates except as follows. *Unsupervised (Family Administration)* — For estates with only personal property less than $60,000 if all claims are determined and those who could take major shares are spouse, issue, parents and grandparents. *Summary* — For estates (minus exempt property) less than $25,000. *Administration Unnecessary* — For estates with only personal property less than cost of the funeral and last 60 days of final illness.
Spouse's Automatic Share: Lifetime use of real estate up to 1/2 acre within municipal limits, 160 acres outside; household furnishings, cars and appliances up to $10,000; personal effects of deceased up to $1,000, and living expenses up to $6,000.
Spouse's Intestate Share: 1) Entire estate if no living issue; 2) $20,000 plus 1/2 balance if living issue are all surviving

spouse's; 3) 1/2 estate if 1 or more living issue are not surviving spouse's.
Spouse's Right of Election: 30% fair market value of estate property in Florida after mortgages, liens and security interests. Estate property may not include jointly held savings and trusts. Must elect within 4 months of first P.R. notice; if will contest places elective share in doubt, elect within 40 days after litigation.
Proving Will: Testimony of 1 signing witness; if unavailable, testimony of P.R. or anyone with knowledge of execution. Self-proved wills accepted.
Nonresident P.R.: Yes, if close relative of deceased.
Notice: *Before P.R Appointment* — No notice required except to those with same or greater right to be P.R. *After P.R. Appointment* — Mail to spouse and those who could take by intestacy or will; promptly publish once a week 2 consecutive weeks. *Summary Administration* — None required except for creditors; promptly publish once a week 2 consecutive weeks.
Forms of Property: Personal property or real estate owned by husband and wife presumes tenancy by entirety and survivorship. Joint tenancy includes survivorship only if stated.
Inventory, Appraisal: Within 60 days of appointment and upon request, present to court. May hire private appraiser.
Claims: Within 3 months of first creditor notice.
P.R. Fees: Reasonable fee.
Attorney Fees: Reasonable fee after informal notice to P.R. and anyone taking an estate share.

GEORGIA: Probate Court
Statutes: Official Code of Georgia Annotated 1982 (Amendments to 1985), Title 53.
Administration: *Supervised* — For all estates except as follows. *Administration Unnecessary* — For solvent estates if property is in-state and those who could take by intestacy or will agree.
Spouse's Automatic Share: Living expenses for at least 1 year; court determines amount and duration.
Spouse's Intestate Share: 1) Entire estate if no living issue; 2) equal share with children if living issue; 3) 1/5 estate if more than 4 shares.
Spouse's Right of Election: No provision.
Proving Will: *Formal Hearing (Solemn Form)*
[Uncontested] — Testimony of 1 signing witness. *[Contested]* — Testimony of all signing witnesses; if out-of-state, insane or in U.S. military, affidavit of anyone proving signature of deceased.

Informal Hearing (Common Form) — Testimony of 1 signing witness; conclusive after 4 years.
Nonresident P.R.: Yes, if post bond twice estate's value.
Notice: ***Before Proving Will*** *[Formal Hearing]* — At least 10 days before hearing, give to spouse and those who could take by will or intestacy if in-state; if identity or address unknown, publish once a week for 4 weeks. Give copy to Probate Clerk to mail to non-residents within 3 days of first publication. *[Informal Hearing]* — None required. ***Before P.R. Appointment*** — Court publishes notice once a week for 4 weeks before hearing. ***After P.R. Appointment****, to Creditors* — Within 60 days of appointment, publish once a week 4 consecutive weeks.
Forms of Property: Tenancy in common presumed unless ownership papers refer to "joint tenants" or similar language. No tenancy by entirety.
Inventory, Appraisal: Within 4 months of P.R. appointment. P.R. may appraise unless court appoints appraiser based on request received within 90 days of filing inventory.
Claims: Within 3 months of last creditor notice.
P.R. Fees: Up to 2.5% of money, 10% of interest on money loaned, 3% of property delivered, 10% of income from real estate handled by P.R. Court may award higher fee.
Attorney Fees: Reasonable fee.

HAWAII: Circuit Court
Statutes: Hawaii Revised Statutes 1976 (Amendments to 1984), Titles 29-30A (Modified UPC).
Administration: ***Supervised*** — For estates more than $40,000 or upon P.R.'s request. ***Unsupervised*** — For estates less than $40,000. ***Summary*** — 1) For estates less than $20,000, court clerk can administer; 2) for estates less than $2,000, court clerk distributes. ***By Affidavit*** — Collect personal property and payment for debts if estate in will is less than $1,000 and no P.R. application is pending.
Spouse's Automatic Share: Homestead up to $5,000; personal property up to $5,000 and living expenses during administration; if estate insolvent, living expenses up to 1 year.
Spouse's Intestate Share: Entire estate if no living issue or parent; otherwise, 1/2 estate.
Spouse's Right of Election: 1/3 estate in will plus 1/3 real estate not in the will if owned by deceased prior to July 1977. Must elect within 9 months of death or 6 months of proving will, whichever is later.
Proving Will: ***Informal Hearing*** — (For estates under $40,000.) Testimony or affidavit of anyone with knowledge of execution. ***Formal Hearing*** *[Uncontested]* — Testimony or affidavit of 1 signing witness. *[Contested]* — Testimony of 1

signing witness; if out-of-state, other evidence. Self-proved wills accepted.
Nonresident P.R.: Yes.
Notice: *Before Proving Will [Formal Hearing]* — At least 14 days before hearing, give or mail to spouse, children, those who could take by intestacy or will and publish once a week 3 consecutive weeks, with last publication at least 10 days before hearing. *[Informal Hearing]* — Same as above except only publish if identity or address unknown. *After P.R. Appointment, to Creditors* — Promptly publish once a week 3 consecutive weeks. If estate less than $10,000, clerk gives notice.
Forms of Property: Tenancy in common presumed unless tenancy by entirety stated. Motor vehicles registered in 2 or more names presumed in joint tenancy. Tenancy by entirety may include cars, leaseholds and shares of corporate stock.
Inventory, Appraisal: Within 30 days of appointment in Supervised Administration; otherwise, at close of administration. Registrar of Wills may hire appraiser if value of property in reasonable doubt.
Claims: Within 4 months of first creditor notice; if no notice, within 3 years of death. If estate less than $10,000, within 60 days of clerk's notice.
P.R. Fees: Up to 4% of first $15,000, 3% of next $85,000, 2% of next $900,000, 1.5% of next $2 million, 1% of balance. Also entitled to 7% of first $5,000 of estate's annual income received while P.R. and 5% of income greater than $5,000. Court may award higher fee.
Attorney Fees: Same as P.R., but no fee based on estate income.

IDAHO: District Court, Magistrates' Division
Statutes: Idaho Code 1979 (Amendments to 1985), Titles 14-15 (UPC).
Administration: *Unsupervised* — For all estates except as follows. *Supervised* — Upon petition, court imposes limited or complete supervision ranging from stopping a sale to continuing control of estate. *Summary* — If spouse is sole inheritor by will or intestacy or estate (minus some real estate claims) totals less than spouse's automatic share and administration, funeral and last-illness costs. *By Affidavit* — Collect personal property and payment for debts if estate is less than $5,000, no P.R. application pending and inheritor applies at least 30 days after death.
Spouse's Automatic Share: 1/2 community property; homestead up to $4,000 if no dependent issue living with spouse, otherwise $10,000; personal property up to $3,500; living expenses up to $500 monthly for 1 year if spouse was supported

by deceased. Court may increase living expenses if P.R. requests.
Spouse's Intestate Share: 1) Entire estate if no living issue or parent; 2) $50,000 plus 1/2 balance if living parent but no living issue or if 1 or more living issue are not surviving spouse's.
Spouse's Right of Election: 1/2 quasi-community property (acquired during marriage while Idaho was not permanent home state), including property transferred to spouse in which deceased retained an interest, and property given to spouse. Must elect within 6 months of first creditor notice unless court extends.
Proving Will: *Formal Hearing [Uncontested]* — Testimony or affidavit of 1 signing witness; if unavailable, other evidence. *[Contested]* — Testimony if witness in-state; otherwise, other evidence. *Informal Hearing* — Testimony or affidavit of anyone with knowledge of execution. Self-proved wills accepted.
Nonresident P.R.: Yes.
Notice: *Before Proving Will [Formal Hearing]* — At least 14 days before hearing, give or mail to those who could take by intestacy or will; if address or identity unknown, publish once a week 3 consecutive weeks, with last publication at least 10 days before hearing. *[Informal Hearing]* — Same as above except only to P.R. and upon request. *After Proving Will [Formal Hearing]* — Not required. *[Informal Hearing]* — If no P.R., mail to those who could take by intestacy or will if addresses reasonably available. *Before P.R. Appointment [Formal Hearing]* — Same as for Before Proving Will except also send to anyone with same or greater right to be P.R. *[Informal Hearing]* — Same as above except only to those with same or greater right to be P.R., upon request and to P.R. *After P.R. Appointment [Formal Hearing]* — None required. *[Informal Hearing]* — Within 30 days mail to those who could take by intestacy or will if address reasonably available. *To Creditors* — Immediately publish once a week 3 consecutive weeks. *Summary Administration* — None required.
Forms of Property: Community property state. Tenancy in common presumed unless joint tenancy stated or property acquired as partnership or community property. Tenancy by entirety not recognized.
Inventory, Appraisal: Within 3 months of appointment. P.R. may hire private appraiser.
Claims: Within 4 months of first creditor notice; if no notice, within 3 years of death.
P.R. Fees: Reasonable fee.
Attorney Fees: Reasonable fee; may need to submit itemization to court.

ILLINOIS: Circuit Court
Statutes: Smith-Hurd Illinois Annotated Statutes 1978 (Amendments to 1985), Ch. 110 1/2, Articles 1-27.
Administration: *Supervised* — If court finds necessary. *Summary* — For estates less than $50,000 if all those who could take by intestacy or will consent and if claims other than those under the will, spouse's automatic share and taxes are arranged. *Administration Unnecessary* — If those who could take by intestacy or will consent and pay taxes and creditors. *By Affidavit* — Collect assets if all who take shares agree and estate is less than $25,000 after claims and funeral expenses.
Spouse's Automatic Share: Living expenses for 9 months up to $10,000 plus $2,000 for each minor child or dependent adult; homestead up to $7,500 if spouse remains on property.
Spouse's Intestate Share: Entire estate if no living issue; otherwise, 1/2 estate.
Spouse's Right of Election: 1/3 estate after debts if surviving issue; otherwise, 1/2 estate. Must elect within 7 months of proving will.
Proving Will: Not required for estates less than $25,000. *Informal Hearing* — Testimony or affidavit of 2 signing witnesses; if insane or unavailable, testimony or affidavit of anyone proving handwriting of witnesses and will's proper execution. *Formal Hearing* — Same as for Informal Hearing if self-proved will is contested within 42 days. Self-proved wills accepted.
Nonresident P.R.: Yes, if named in will and appoint resident agent.
Notice: *Before P.R. Appointment* — At least 30 days before hearing, mail or give to anyone with same or greater right to be P.R. and anyone who can nominate P.R. *After P.R. Appointment* — After 14 days, give or mail to those who could take by intestacy or will; if identity or address unknown, publish 3 consecutive weeks, the first within less than 14 days of appointment. *Before Summary Administration Hearing* — At least 30 days before hearing, publish once a week 3 consecutive weeks.
Forms of Property: Tenancy in common presumed. Joint tenancy with right of survivorship created only by declaration that estate, including personal property, is in joint tenancy and not tenancy in common. No tenancy by entirety.
Inventory, Appraisal: Within 60 days of appointment. P.R. may hire private appraiser.
Claims: Within 6 months of appointment or creditor notice, whichever is later.
P.R. Fees: Reasonable fee.
Attorney Fees: Reasonable fee.

INDIANA: Circuit Court, Superior Court; Probate Court in St. Joseph's County
Statutes: West's Annotated Indiana Code 1979 (Amendments to 1985), Title 29 (Modified UPC).
Administration: *Unsupervised* — For solvent estates if all who could take by intestacy or will agree. *Supervised* — At court's discretion or upon request. *Summary* — If estate (minus some real estate claims) totals less than spouse's automatic share plus administration, funeral costs. *By Affidavit* — Spouse collects car(s) at least 5 days after death, other assets for estates less than $8,500 at least 45 days after death if no P.R. application pending.
Spouse's Automatic Share: Personal property up to $8,500; real estate to make up the difference if less than $8,500 in personal property.
Spouse's Intestate Share: 1) Entire estate if no living issue or parent; 2) 3/4 estate after debts if living parent but no living issue; 3) 1/2 estate after debts if 1 living child or living issue of 1 deceased child; 4) 1/3 estate after debts if 2 or more living children, or if 1 living child and living issue of 1 or more deceased children, or living issue of 2 or more deceased children; 5) lifetime use of 1/3 real estate and intestate share if surviving spouse is not first spouse, is childless by deceased and deceased has living child from previous marriage.
Spouse's Right of Election: 1/3 personal property after debts and lifetime use of 1/3 land if surviving spouse is not first spouse, is childless by deceased and deceased has living children from previous marriage; otherwise, 1/3 estate. Must elect within 6 months of 2nd publication of creditor notice; if will contested, within 30 days after litigation ends.
Proving Will: Testimony or affidavit of 1 signing witness; some courts require testimony. If out-of-state or insane, by proving handwriting of deceased or 2 signing witnesses. Self-proved wills accepted.
Nonresident P.R.: Yes, if file bond and appoint resident agent.
Notice: *After P.R. Appointment* — Probate Court Clerk publishes once a week 2 consecutive weeks. P.R. must prepare envelopes for clerk to mail to those who could take by intestacy and will if name and address known. *Summary Administration* — None required.
Forms of Property: Joint tenancy, tenancy in common and tenancy by entirety recognized. For real estate jointly owned (except by married couple), tenancy in common presumed unless joint tenancy stated. Joint ownership by husband and wife presumes tenancy by entirety.
Inventory, Appraisal: Within 2 months after appointment. P.R. may hire private appraiser.

Claims: Within 5 months of first creditor notice, 3 months after closing statement for Unsupervised Administration or 3 months after court revokes will naming claimant.
P.R. Fees: Reasonable fee.
Attorney Fees: Reasonable fee.

IOWA: District Court
Statutes: Iowa Code Annotated 1964 (Amendments to 1986), Title 32, Ch. 633.
Administration: *Supervised* — For all estates except as follows. *Administration Unnecessary* — For solvent estates less than $15,000 if inheritors by intestacy or will are spouse, children or parents and no P.R. application is pending.
Spouse's Automatic Share: Living expenses for 1 year and certain personal property.
Spouse's Intestate Share: 1) Entire estate if no living issue or all living issue are also surviving spouse's; 2) entire estate including spouse's automatic share up to $50,000 or 1/2 estate over $50,000 if 1 or more living issue are not surviving spouse's.
Spouse's Right of Election: 1/3 real estate owned by deceased during marriage and 1/3 personal property after debts. May elect lifetime use of home instead. Must elect within 4 months of 2nd creditor publication.
Proving Will: Testimony or affidavit of 1 signing witness; if unavailable, 2 witnesses proving handwriting of deceased and signing witnesses. Self-proved wills accepted.
Nonresident P.R.: Yes, but must have resident co-P.R. unless court approves serving alone.
Notice: *Before Probate Hearing* — At court's discretion.
After P.R. Appointment — Promptly publish once a week 2 consecutive weeks. *Administration Unnecessary* — Clerk publishes notice.
Forms of Property: Tenancy in common presumed unless joint tenancy stated. No tenancy by entirety.
Inventory, Appraisal: Within 90 days of appointment. Appraisal only upon request.
Claims: Within 4 months of 2nd publication of P.R. appointment.
P.R. Fees: Up to 6% of first $1,000, 4% of next $4,000, 2% over $5,000. Court may award higher fee.
Attorney Fees: Same as P.R.

KANSAS: District Court
Statutes: Kansas Statutes Annotated 1983 (Amendments to 1986), Ch. 59.
Administration: *Unsupervised (Simplified)* — For all estates except as follows. *Supervised* — At court's discretion

or upon request. **Summary** — If estate (minus spouse's automatic share) is less than debts plus last-illness, funeral and administration costs. **Administration Unnecessary (Refusal to Grant Letters)** — For estates with only personal property less than $10,000 if creditor applies and no surviving spouse or child, or for all estates if taxes paid and court finds administration unnecessary.

Spouse's Automatic Share: Personal property or cash up to $7,500 plus lifetime use of real estate up to 1 acre within municipal limits, 60 acres outside if no taxes owed.

Spouse's Intestate Share: Entire estate if no living issue; otherwise, 1/2 estate.

Spouse's Right of Election: Intestate share. Must elect within 6 months of proving will.

Proving Will: Testimony of 2 signing witnesses; if unavailable, testimony of anyone with knowledge of execution and of signatures of witnesses and deceased. Self-proved wills accepted.

Nonresident P.R.: Yes, if named in will and appoint resident agent.

Notice: *Before Proving Will, P.R. Appointment* — Within 7 days of first creditor publication, mail to those who could take by intestacy or will for Administration Unnecessary, Unsupervised Administration, if no will or if surviving spouse contests will. *To Creditors* — Publish once a week 3 consecutive weeks.

Forms of Property: Tenancy in common presumed unless joint tenancy stated and transfer is from sole owner to recipient and 1 other. No tenancy by entirety.

Inventory, Appraisal: Within 30 days of P.R. appointment. P.R. must hire court-approved appraiser if requested.

Claims: Within 4 months of first creditor notice. Within 9 months of death for Administration Unnecessary.

P.R. Fees: Reasonable fee.

Attorney Fees: Reasonable fee.

KENTUCKY: District Court

Statutes: Baldwin's Kentucky Revised Statutes Annotated, 4th Ed., 1969 (Amendments to 1986), Title 32, Ch. 391-397.

Administration: *Supervised* — For all estates except as follows. *Administration Unnecessary* — For solvent estates if those who could take by intestacy or will agree; for estates less than $5,000 if surviving spouse applies.

Spouse's Automatic Share: 1/2 community property including out-of-state personal property, 1/2 real estate owned at death, lifetime use of other real estate, 1/2 separate personal property and living expenses up to $7,500 after administration,

funeral and last-illness costs.
Spouse's Intestate Share: Entire estate if no living issue, parents, siblings or issue of deceased siblings; otherwise, same as automatic share.
Spouse's Right of Election: Same as automatic share except 1/3 real estate limit. Must elect within 6 months of proving will.
Proving Will: *Uncontested* — Testimony of 1 signing witness; if at least 50 miles away, then by affidavit; if out-of-state or insane, testimony of 2 witnesses proving handwriting of deceased and other evidence. Self proved wills accepted.
Contested — At court's discretion.
Nonresident P.R.: Yes, if related to deceased.
Notice: *Before P.R. Appointment* — Mail at least 5 days before hearing to spouse and residents who could take by intestacy. Publish once a week 6 consecutive weeks for Administration Unnecessary. For estates less than $5,000, court may eliminate notice. *After P.R. Appointment Hearing, to Creditors* — Clerk publishes at least once a month for 1 year.
Forms of Property: Tenancy in common presumed between husband and wife unless joint tenancy stated. Tenancy by entirety recognized in personal property.
Inventory, Appraisal: Within 2 months of appointment. P.R. may hire private appraiser.
Claims: Within 1 year of appointment; if no P.R., within 3 years of death.
P.R. Fees: Up to 5% of personal property plus 5% of all estate income collected by P.R.
Attorney Fees: Reasonable fee.

LOUISIANA: District Court
Statutes: West's Louisiana Statutes Annotated 1961 (Amendments to 1986), Code of Civil Procedure, Articles 2811-3462; Civil Code, Articles 871-1465.
Administration: *Supervised* — For all estates except as follows. *Administration Unnecessary* — 1) For estates less than $50,000 if the only inheritors are spouse, siblings or issue; 2) for all estates if creditors consent and inheritors accept liability for debts.
Spouse's Automatic Share: 1/2 community property. If surviving spouse's estate is worth 1/5 or less of deceased's estate, then also gets 1) 1/4 estate if no child; 2) lifetime use of 1/4 estate until remarriage if 3 or fewer children 3) lifetime use of share equal to children's if 4 or more children.
Spouse's Intestate Share: 1) Entire estate if no living issue or parent; 2) 1/2 estate if living parent but no living issue; 3) lifetime use of deceased's separate property until remarriage if

Appendix I

issue.
Spouse's Right of Election: No provision.
Proving Will: 1) Statutory Will (see Note) — Testimony of notary and 1 witness or 2 signing witnesses; if unavailable, testimony of 2 witnesses proving testator's handwriting. 2) Mystic and Nuncupative Wills (See Note) — Testimony of at least 3 signing witnesses; if witnesses out-of-state, testimony of in-state witnesses; if unavailable, testimony of 2 witnesses who recognize signature of deceased or notary. Self-proved wills accepted.
Nonresident P.R.: Yes, if appoint resident agent.
Notice: *Before P.R. Appointment* — None required except if requested within 10 days of death. *After P.R. Appointment, to Creditors* — At court's discretion.
Forms of Property: Community property state. Joint ownership (indivision) if 2 or more persons listed as owners. No tenancy by entirety or tenancy in common.
Inventory, Appraisal: Only if requested by inheritor; if inheritor accepts share without inventory and appraisal, inheritor is responsible for all estate debts, not only claims on inherited share. Court may order 3 public appraisers.
Claims: Before or at final hearing, but usually can be submitted up to 3 years later.
P.R. Fees: Up to 2.5% of inventory. Court may award higher fee.
Attorney Fees: No statutory provision.
Notes: Louisiana recognizes 3 types of wills: mystic (3 witnesses to notarization, will sealed in envelope); nuncupative (public — read aloud in front of 3 witnesses and a notary, or private — notary must witness signing); statutory (2 witnesses). Upon death, some relatives inherit property automatically and can only reject personal liability for debts of the deceased by rejecting the inheritance.

MAINE: Probate Court
Statutes: Maine Revised Statutes Annotated 1964 (Amendments to 1985), Title 18A, Sections 1-101 to 8-401; Maine Rules of Court 1986, Rule 4, (UPC).
Administration: *Unsupervised (Independent)* — For all estates except as follows. *Supervised* — Upon petition, court imposes limited or complete supervision ranging from stopping a sale to continuing control of estate. *Summary* — If estate (minus some real estate claims) totals less than spouse's automatic share and administration, funeral, last-illness costs. *By Affidavit* — Collect personal property and payment for debts for estates less than $10,000 if at least 30 days after death and no P.R. application is pending.
Spouse's Automatic Share: Homestead up to $5,000,

personal property up to $3,500 and living expenses during administration; if estate insolvent, living expenses up to 1 year.
Spouse's Intestate Share: 1) Entire estate if no living issue or parent; 2) $50,000 plus 1/2 balance if living parent but no living issue, or living issue are all surviving spouse's; 3) 1/2 estate if 1 or more living issue are not surviving spouse's.
Spouse's Right of Election: 1/3 estate (which includes gifts and joint property).
Proving Will: *Informal Hearing* — Testimony or affidavit of anyone with knowledge of execution. *Formal Hearing [Uncontested]* — Testimony or affidavit of 1 signing witness if in-state; if unavailable, other evidence. *[Contested]* — Testimony of 1 signing witness if in-state; if unavailable, other evidence. Self-proved wills accepted.
Nonresident P.R.: Yes.
Notice: *Before Proving Will [Formal Hearing]* — Court sets method to notify spouse, children, those who could take by intestacy or any will and those who request it. *[Informal Hearing]* — Same as above, only upon request. *Before P.R. Appointment [Formal Hearing]* — Same as for Formal Hearing Before Proving Will, except also to anyone with the same or greater right to be P.R.; publish as court orders. *[Informal Hearing]* — Same as above, except publication not required. *After P.R. Appointment* — If notice not already given, mail to all who could take by intestacy or will if address available. *To Creditors* — Publish once a week 2 consecutive weeks.
Forms of Property: Ownership by 2 or more presumed tenancy in common unless joint tenancy stated. No tenancy by entirety.
Inventory, Appraisal: Within 3 months of appointment. P.R. must hire private appraiser for real estate and securities not regularly traded on recognized exchange.
Claims: Within 4 months of first published notice.
P.R. Fees: Reasonable fee.
Attorney Fees: Reasonable fee.

MARYLAND: Orphans' Court; Montgomery and Hartford Counties, Circuit Court
Statutes: Annotated Code of the Public General Laws of Maryland 1974 (Amendments to 1985), Estates & Trusts, Titles 1-12.
Administration: *Supervised* — For all estates except as follows. *Summary* — For estates less than $10,000.
Spouse's Automatic Share: Living expenses up to $2,000, plus $1,000 for each child under 18.
Spouse's Intestate Share: 1) Entire estate if no living issue or parent; 2) 1/2 estate if living child under 18; 3) $15,000 plus 1/2 balance if living issue is not child under 18 or living parent but

no living issue.
Spouse's Right of Election: 1/3 estate after debts if living issue; otherwise, 1/2 estate. Must elect within 30 days after claims due.
Proving Will: *Informal Hearing (Abbreviated)* — Affidavit or testimony of anyone with knowledge of execution. *Formal Hearing (Judicial)* — Upon request or court order; court determines method. Self-proved wills accepted.
Nonresident P.R.: Yes, if appoint resident agent.
Notice: *Before Proving Will [Formal Hearing]* — If hearing requested, notify registrar, who will mail to those named in filed papers and publish once a week 2 consecutive weeks. *[Informal Hearing]* — None required. *After P.R. Appointment* — Within 20 days, mail registrar text of creditor notice and names and addresses of those who could take by intestacy or will. Registrar will publish once a week 2 consecutive weeks.
Forms of Property: Tenancy in common recognized. Joint tenancy must be stated. Joint ownership by spouses presumes tenancy by entirety unless stated otherwise.
Inventory, Appraisal: Within 3 months of appointment. P.R. may appraise assets when face value equals cash value; otherwise, by court-appointed appraiser.
Claims: Within 6 months of P.R. appointment; 1 day extension for each day notice is late.
P.R. Fees: Up to 10% of first $20,000; 4% over $20,000; limit of 10% of real estate sold.
Attorney Fees: Reasonable fee.

MASSACHUSETTS: District Court, Probate and Family Departments
Statutes: Annotated Laws of Massachusetts 1981 (Amendments to 1986), Part II, Title II, Ch. 189-206.
Administration: *Supervised* — For all estates except as follows. *Summary (Informal)* — For estates with only personal property less than $5,000 (excluding motor vehicle) if surviving spouse, child, grandchild, parent, sibling or their children applies at least 30 days after death, and no P.R. application is pending.
Spouse's Automatic Share: Living expenses and use of home for 6 months. In some cases, use of homestead up to $100,000 until death or remarriage.
Spouse's Intestate Share: 1) Entire estate if no living issue, parent, sibling, first cousins or their issue; 2) entire estate if less than $50,000; otherwise, $50,000 plus 1/2 balance if no living issue but other living relatives; 3) 1/2 estate if living issue.
Spouse's Right of Election: 1) 1/3 estate if issue; 2) $25,000 plus 1/2 balance of personal property in trust, and 1/2

balance of real estate for lifetime use if no living issue but relatives; 3) $25,000 plus 1/2 estate if no issue or relatives. Instead, may elect lifetime use of 1/3 real estate (Dower). Must elect within 6 months after proving will.
Proving Will: Testimony or affidavit of 1 signing witness; no proof necessary if written consent by spouse, relatives and all who could take by will or intestacy. Self-proved wills accepted.
Nonresident P.R.: Yes, if appoint resident agent.
Notice: *Before Proving Will, P.R. Appointment* — Mail or give to surviving spouse, all who could take by intestacy or will and publish once a week 2 consecutive weeks. Court may require earlier notice. No notice necessary if no will or if court and all in-state relatives agree. *After Proving Will, P.R. Appointment* — Within 3 months, mail to all who could take by intestacy or will if addresses known. No notice to creditors unless estate is insolvent.
Forms of Property: Tenancy in common, joint tenancy and tenancy by entirety recognized. Joint ownership by husband and wife creates joint tenancy.
Inventory, Appraisal: Within 3 months of appointment. P.R. must hire private appraiser for real estate.
Claims: Within 4 months of P.R. posting bond.
P.R. Fees: No provision.
Attorney Fees: No provision.

MICHIGAN: Probate Court
Statutes: Michigan Statutes Annotated 1980 (Amendments to 1986), Ch. 27-5001-27.5993; Michigan Compiled Laws 1980 (Amendments to 1986), 700.1- 749; Michigan Court Rules 1985, (Probate Court).
Administration: *Unsupervised (Independent)* — For all estates except as follows. *Supervised* — Upon petition or at court's discretion, court will impose limited or complete supervision ranging from stopping a sale to continuing control of estate. *Summary* — If estate (minus some real estate claims) totals less than spouse's automatic share and administration, funeral and last-illness costs; for estates less than $5,000 after funeral expenses if surviving spouse applies. If no spouse, next inheritor.
Spouse's Automatic Share: Homestead up to $10,000; personal property up to $3,500; living expenses through administration or 1 year, whichever is earlier.
Spouse's Intestate Share: 1) Entire estate if no surviving issue or parent; 2) $60,000 and 1/2 balance of estate if living parent but no issue or living issue are all surviving spouse's; 3) 1/2 estate if 1 or more living issue are not surviving spouse's.
Spouse's Right of Election: 1/2 estate (which includes 1/2

certain gifts from deceased and joint property) or lifetime use of 1/3 real estate owned during marriage (Dower). Must elect within 60 days of deadline for claims or inventory, whichever is later.
Proving Will: Testimony or affidavit of 1 signing witness; if out-of-state, testimony of witnesses to will's execution or by proof of handwriting of deceased and witnesses. *Unsupervised (Independent)* — Will presumed valid if has required signatures; otherwise, affidavit of anyone with knowledge of execution. Self-proved wills accepted.
Nonresident P.R.: Yes.
Notice: *Before Proving Will, P.R. Appointment* — Mail 14 days or give 7 days before hearing to those who could take by intestacy or will. If address unknown, publish once at least 14 days before hearing. *After Proving Will Unsupervised (Independent)* — Within 10 days, mail or give copy of petition and will to those who could take by intestacy or will if address known. *To Creditors* — Publish once at least 4 months before closing estate; may publish before P.R. appointment. *Summary Administration* — None required.
Forms of Property: Tenancy in common, joint tenancy, tenancy by entirety recognized. Joint tenancy created only if stated. Joint tenancy by spouses and joint ownership of real estate by spouses presumed tenancy by entirety unless otherwise stated. Joint tenancy with right of survivorship recognized for bank accounts, securities and safe deposit box contents, but must be in writing.
Inventory, Appraisal: Within 90 days. P.R. may hire private appraiser. *Supervised Administration* — Within 60 days. P.R. must hire court-appointed appraiser.
Claims: Within 2-4 months of creditor publication.
P.R. Fees: Reasonable fee.
Attorney Fees: Reasonable fee.

MINNESOTA: Probate Court
Statutes: Minnesota Statutes Annotated 1975 (Amendments to 1986), Ch. 524-528.
Administration: *Unsupervised* — For all estates except as follows. *Supervised* — Upon petition, court imposes limited or complete supervision ranging from stopping a sale to continuing control of estate. *Summary* — If estate (minus some real estate claims) totals less than spouse's automatic share and administration, funeral and last-illness costs, if estate (excluding homestead) is less than $30,000, or if estate is insolvent.
Administration Unnecessary (Unsupervised Summary) — If estate (minus some real estate claims) is less than spouse's automatic share and administration, funeral and last-illness costs. *By Affidavit* — Collect property if estate less than $5,000, inheritor applies at least 30 days after death,

and no P.R. application is pending.
Spouse's Automatic Share: Personal property up to $9,000, 1 automobile, living expenses during administration up to 18 months for solvent estates or 12 months for insolvent, plus homestead or lifetime use of homestead if living children or issue of deceased children.
Spouse's Intestate Share: 1) Entire estate if no living issue; 2) $70,000 and 1/2 balance if living issue are all surviving spouse's; 3) 1/2 estate if 1 or more living issue not surviving spouse's.
Spouse's Right of Election: 1/3 estate (which includes certain gifts to surviving spouse). Must elect within 9 months of death or 6 months after proving will, whichever is later.
Proving Will: *Informal Hearing* — Testimony or affidavit of anyone with knowledge of execution. *Formal Hearing [Uncontested]* — Testimony or affidavit of 1 signing witness; if unavailable, other evidence; *[Contested]* — Testimony of 1 signing witness or other evidence. Self-proved wills accepted.
Nonresident P.R.: Yes.
Notice: *Before Proving Will, P.R. Appointment [Formal Hearing]* — At least 14 days before hearing, mail to spouse, children, creditor, those who could take by intestacy or will, anyone named P.R. in any will or with same or greater right to be P.R. At least 10 days before hearing, publish once a week 2 consecutive weeks. *[Informal Hearing]* — Same as above; mail only upon request to anyone with same or greater right to be P.R. *After Proving Will, P.R. Appointment, to Creditors* — Publish once a week 2 consecutive weeks under clerk's direction. *[Informal Hearing]* — Same as for creditors, except mail also to those who could take by intestacy or will. *Before Spouse's Election Hearing* — Same as Before Proving Will, except mail only to those who would otherwise inherit property.
Forms of Property: Tenancy in common presumed unless joint tenancy in writing. No tenancy by entirety.
Inventory, Appraisal: Due 3 months after appointment. P.R. may hire private appraiser.
Claims: Within 4 months of first published notice.
P.R. Fees: Reasonable fee.
Attorney Fees: Reasonable fee.

MISSISSIPPI: Chancery Court
Statutes: Mississippi Code Annotated 1972 (Amendments to 1985), Title 91.
Administration: *Supervised* — For all estates except as follows. *By Affidavit* — Collect personal property and payment for debts for estates less than $10,000 if surviving spouse (if no

spouse, next inheritor) applies at least 30 days after death and no P.R. application is pending.
Spouse's Automatic Share: Lifetime use of homestead up to $30,000 and 150 acres, plus living expenses for 1 year.
Spouse's Intestate Share: Entire estate if no surviving issue; otherwise, take equal shares with children.
Spouse's Right of Election: 1) 1/2 estate (which includes joint property) if no issue; 2) 1/3 estate (which includes joint property) if issue; 3) nothing if surviving spouse's property equals intestate share. Must elect within 90 days of proving will.
Proving Will: Testimony of 1 signing witness; if dead or insane, by proving handwriting of deceased and signing witnesses. Self-proved wills accepted.
Nonresident P.R.: Yes.
Notice: *After P.R. Appointment* — Within 90 days, publish 3 consecutive weeks in general circulation newspaper; if unavailable, post at courthouse and in 3 other public places in county; for estates less than $500, post 30 days at courthouse and 2 other public places.
Forms of Property: Tenancy in common, joint tenancy and tenancy by entirety recognized. Ownership by 2 or more persons presumes tenancy in common unless joint tenancy stated.
Inventory, Appraisal: Within 90 days of appointment. P.R. must hire court-appointed appraiser for all property except money and debts.
Claims: Within 90 days of first creditor notice.
P.R. Fees: 1% to 7% of estate at court's discretion, plus expenses. No fee on estate profit not normally estate income.
Attorney Fees: Reasonable fee.

MISSOURI: Circuit Court (Probate Divison)
Statutes: Vernon's Annotated Missouri Statutes 1956 (Amendments to 1986), Ch. 472-474 (Modified UPC).
Administration: *Unsupervised* — If will directs or all inheritors by intestacy or will agree. *Supervised* — Upon petition, court imposes limited or complete supervision ranging from stopping a sale to continuing control of estate.
Administration Unnecessary (Refusal of Letters) — 1) For estates less than spouse's automatic share if spouse or unmarried minor children apply; 2) if no surviving spouse or child, estate is less than $5,000, creditor applies and posts bond; 3) for estates less than $15,000 if inheritor files affidavit at least 30 days after death and no P.R. application is pending.
Spouse's Automatic Share: Some personal property, reasonable living expenses for 1 year and homestead up to 1/2 estate or $7,500, whichever is less.
Spouse's Intestate Share: 1) Entire estate if no living issue or parent; 2) $20,000 and 1/2 balance if living parent but no issue

or living issue are all surviving spouse's; 3) 1/2 estate if 1 or more living issue are not surviving spouse's.
Spouse's Right of Election: 1/2 estate if no issue; otherwise, 1/3 estate. Must elect within 6 months and 10 days after first creditor notice.
Proving Will: Testimony of 2 signing witnesses; if dead or insane, testimony of available signing witness and proof of other witnesses' handwriting; if witness unavailable, other evidence. Self-proved wills accepted.
Nonresident P.R.: Yes, if appoint resident agent.
Notice: *After P.R. Appointment* — Upon appointment, clerk publishes notice once a week 4 consecutive weeks and mails copy to those named in court records.
Forms of Property: Tenancy in common, joint tenancy and tenancy by entirety recognized. Ownership by 2 or more persons presumes tenancy in common unless joint tenancy stated.
Inventory, Appraisal: Within 30 days of appointment. P.R. may hire private appraiser.
Claims: Within 6 months of first publication notice; if no notice given, within 3 years of death.
P.R. Fees: Up to 5% of first $5,000, 4% of next $20,000, 3% of next $75,000, 2.75% of next $300,000, 2.5% of next $600,000, 2% of amount over $1 million. Court may award higher fee.
Attorney Fees: Same as P.R., except attorney who acts as P.R. may collect fee only once.

MONTANA: District Court
Statutes: Montana Code Annotated 1985, Title 72 (UPC).
Administration: *Unsupervised* — For all estates except as follows. *Supervised* — Upon petition, court imposes limited or complete supervision ranging from stopping a sale to continuing control of estate. *Summary* — If estate, after debts, totals less than $7,500 or if estate (minus some real estate claims) totals less than living expenses, exempt property, administration, funeral and last-illness costs.
Spouse's Automatic Share: Homestead up to $20,000, personal property up to $3,500 and living expenses during administration; if estate insolvent, living expenses up to 1 year.
Spouse's Intestate Share: 1) Entire estate if no living issue or if living issue are all issue of surviving spouse; 2) 1/2 estate if 1 or more living issue is not surviving spouse's; 3) 1/3 estate if more than 1 living child or 1 child and issue of 1 or more deceased children who are not surviving spouse's.
Spouse's Right of Election: 1/3 estate (which includes gifts and joint property). Must elect within 9 months of death with some exceptions.
Proving Will: *Informal Hearing* — Testimony or affidavit of anyone with knowledge of execution. *Formal Hearing*

[Uncontested]— Testimony or affidavit of 1 signing witness or other evidence. *[Contested]*— Testimony of 1 signing witness; if out-of-state or insane, other evidence.
Nonresident P.R.: Yes.
Notice: *Before Proving Will [Formal Hearing]*— At least 14 days before hearing, give or mail notice to spouse, children, those who could take by intestacy or by any will offered, and P.R.; if name or address unknown, publish 3 times with at least 10 days and not more than 3 weeks between first and last publications. *[Informal Hearing]*— Same as above, except only to P.R. and upon request. *Before P.R. Appointment [Formal Hearing]*— Same as Before Proving Will except also to creditors and anyone with property claims or with same or greater right to be P.R. *[Informal Hearing]*— Same as above except only to those with equal or greater right to be P.R. and upon request. *After P.R. Appointment*— Within 30 days, give or mail notice to those who could take by intestacy or will. *To Creditors*— Upon appointment, publish once a week 3 consecutive weeks.
Summary Administration — None required.
Forms of Property: Partnership interests, tenancy in common, joint tenancy (called "interests in common" and "joint interests") recognized. No tenancy by entirety in personal property.
Inventory, Appraisal: Within 3 months of appointment. P.R. must hire private appraiser.
Claims: Within 4 months of first creditor notice; if no notice given, within 3 years of death.
P.R. Fees: Reasonable fee up to 3% of first $40,000, 2% of amount over $40,000. P.R. entitled to minimum fee of $100 or value of estate, whichever is less.
Attorney Fees: Up to 1.5 times allowable P.R. fee. Court may award higher fee.

NEBRASKA: County Court
Statutes: Revised Statutes of Nebraska 1943 (Amendments to 1985), Ch. 30 (UPC).
Administration: *Unsupervised*— For all estates except as follows. *Supervised* — Upon petition, court imposes limited or complete supervision ranging from stopping a sale to continuing control of estate. *Summary* — If estate (minus some real estate claims) totals less than allowances, administration, funeral and last-illness costs. *By Affidavit*— Collect personal property if estate (minus some real estate claims) totals less than $10,000, if inheritor applies at least 30 days after death and no P.R. application is pending.
Spouse's Automatic Share: Homestead up to $5,000; personal property up to $5,000; living expenses during administration; if estate insolvent, living expenses up to 1 year.

Spouse's Intestate Share: 1) Entire estate if no living issue or parent; 2) $50,000 plus 1/2 balance if living parent but no living issue, or if living issue are all surviving spouse's; 3) 1/2 estate if all living issue are not surviving spouse's.
Spouse's Right of Election: 1/3 estate (which includes gifts and joint property). Must elect within 9 months of death or 6 months of proving will, whichever is later.
Proving Will: *Informal* — Testimony or affidavit of anyone with knowledge of execution. *Formal [Uncontested]* — Testimony or affidavit of 1 signing witness; if unavailable, other evidence. *[Contested]* — Testimony of 1 signing witness; if out-of-state or insane, other evidence. Self-proved wills accepted.
Nonresident P.R.: Yes.
Notice: *Before Proving Will [Formal Hearing]* — At least 14 days before hearing, give or mail to those named in will, spouse, children and P.R. named in any will. Clerk publishes once a week 3 consecutive weeks at least 3 days before hearing. *[Informal Hearing]* — Same as above, except only upon request and to P.R. *Before P.R. Appointment [Formal Hearing]* — Same as Before Proving Will, except also to anyone with same or greater right to be P.R. *[Informal Hearing]* — Same as above except only to anyone with equal or greater right to be P.R. *After P.R. Appointment, to Creditors* — If notice not already given, within 30 days of P.R. appointment clerk publishes once a week 3 consecutive weeks. *Informal* — Within 5 days of first publication, give or mail to spouse, children, those named in will and anyone with same or greater right to be P.R. *Summary Administration* — None required.
Forms of Property: Tenancy in common and joint tenancy recognized. No tenancy by entirety.
Inventory, Appraisal: Within 2 months of appointment. P.R. may hire private appraiser.
Claims: Within 2 months of first creditor notice.
P.R. Fees: Reasonable fee.
Attorney Fees: Reasonable fee.

NEVADA: District Court
Statutes: Nevada Revised Statutes 1985, Title 12, Ch. 132-156.
Administration: Supervised (Formal) — For all estates except as follows. ***Summary*** — For estates less than $100,000 if court agrees. ***Administration Unnecessary*** — At court's discretion for estates less than $25,000 if spouse or child applies. ***By Affidavit*** — Collect all property for estates less than $10,000 with no real estate if surviving spouse, children, issue of deceased children, parent or sibling apply at least 40 days after death and no P.R. application is pending.
Spouse's Automatic Share: 1/2 community property plus

homestead, some personal property and, at court's discretion, living expenses.
Spouse's Intestate Share: 1) Entire separate estate if no living issue, parent or sibling; 2) 1/2 separate estate if only 1 living child or living issue of 1 deceased child, or living parent or sibling but no living issue; 3) 1/3 estate if more than 1 living child or 1 living child and living issue of deceased child.
Spouse's Right of Election: No provision.
Proving Will: *Uncontested* — Testimony or affidavit of 1 signing witness; if dead, insane, in the armed forces or otherwise unavailable, testimony or affidavit of 2 witnesses proving signature of deceased or other evidence. *Contested* — Testimony of all signing witnesses; if insane, dead or out of the country, other evidence. Self-proved wills accepted.
Nonresident P.R.: No.
Notice: *Before Proving Will, P.R. Appointment* — At least 10 days before hearing, give or mail to those who could take by intestacy or will, P.R. and upon request. Publish 3 times with at least 10 days and no more than 3 weeks between first and last publication. *Before Summary Administration* — For estates less than $25,000, at least 10 days before hearing mail to those who could take by intestacy or will, upon request and to P.R. *By Affidavit* — At least 10 days before collecting property, mail to those with same or greater right to property. *After P.R. Appointment, to Creditors* — Upon appointment, publish as Before Proving Will.
Forms of Property: Community property state. Tenancy in common, joint tenancy and community property recognized. No tenancy by entirety.
Inventory, Appraisal: Within 60 days of appointment. P.R. may hire private appraiser.
Claims: Within 90 days of first creditor notice; if estate less than $60,000, within 60 days; if no notice given, before final accounting.
P.R. Fees: Up to 6% of first $1,000, 4% of next $4,000, 2% of balance. Court may award higher fee.
Attorney Fees: Reasonable fee if submit application detailing 1) time and hours, 2) nature and extent of services, 3) ordinary and extraordinary expenses and 4) complexity of work.

NEW HAMPSHIRE: Probate Court
Statutes: New Hampshire Revised Statutes Annotated 1974 (Amendments to 1985), Titles 56-57, Ch. 547-569.
Administration: *Supervised* — For all estates except as follows. *Summary* — For estates less than $2,000.

Spouse's Automatic Share: Use of home and living expenses for 40 days after death. Living expenses during administration deducted from inherited share.
Spouse's Intestate Share: 1) Entire estate if no living issue or parent; 2) $50,000 and 1/2 balance if living parent or living issue are all surviving spouse's; 3) 1/2 estate if 1 or more living issue are not surviving spouse's.
Spouse's Right of Election: 1) 1/3 estate if living issue; 2) $10,000 personal property, $10,000 real estate and 1/2 balance if no living issue, but living parents or siblings; 3) $10,000, 1/2 balance and $2,000 for each full year of marriage if no living issue, parents or siblings. Must elect within 6 months of P.R. appointment.
Proving Will: *Informal Hearing (Common Form)* — Testimony of 1 signing witness; if unavailable, other evidence. *Formal Hearing (Solemn Form)* — Testimony of 3 signing witnesses; if unavailable, other evidence. Self-proved wills accepted.
Nonresident P.R.: No, with court-approved exceptions.
Notice: *After Proving Will* — Within 60 days after proving will, give or mail to those who could take by intestacy or will. *To Creditors* — Within 15 days, pay registrar to publish 2 consecutive weeks.
Forms of Property: Tenancy in common presumed unless joint tenancy stated. Ownership by spouses creates joint tenancy. No tenancy by entirety.
Inventory, Appraisal: Within 3 months of P.R. appointment. P.R. must hire 1 court-appointed appraiser for estates less than $2,000; otherwise, 3 court-appointed appraisers.
Claims: Within 6 months of P.R. appointment.
P.R. Fees: Reasonable fee.
Attorney Fees: Reasonable fee.

NEW JERSEY: Surrogate or Superior Court
Statutes: New Jersey Statutes Annotated, 1983 (Amendments to 1986), Title 3B 1-29.
Administration: *Unsupervised* — For all estates except as follows. *Administration Unnecessary* — For estates less than $10,000 if surviving spouse applies; estates less than $5,000 if no living spouse and next inheritor applies with consent of all other inheritors.
Spouse's Automatic Share: No provision.
Spouse's Intestate Share: 1) Entire estate if no living issue or parent; 2) $50,000 and 1/2 balance if living parent or living issue are all surviving spouse's; 3) 1/2 estate if 1 or more living issue are not surviving spouse's.
Spouse's Right of Election: 1/3 estate (which includes certain gifts and joint property) or lifetime use of 1/2 real estate

owned during marriage after January 1, 1929, and before May 28, 1980 (Dower). Must elect within 6 months of proving will.
Proving Will: *Informal Hearing (Common Form)* — Testimony of 1 signing witness or anyone with knowledge of execution; if out-of-state, affidavit, if incompetent or dead, other evidence. *Formal Hearing (Solemn Form)* — Testimony of at least 1 signing witness, but court may require 2; if out-of-state, affidavit; if incompetent or dead, other evidence. Self-proved wills accepted.
Nonresident P.R.: Yes, if post bond.
Notice: *Before Proving Will* — At least 10 days (in-state) or 60 days (out-of-state) before hearing, mail to those with same or greater right to be P.R. *After Proving Will* — Within 60 days, mail to those in will. *To Creditors* — Within 20 days of court order, publish once a week 2 consecutive weeks.
Forms of Property: Tenancy in common, joint tenancy and tenancy by entirety recognized. Ownership by spouses presumes tenancy by entirety unless stated otherwise. Tenancy by entirety not recognized for personal property.
Inventory, Appraisal: Not required unless court directs or spouse requests personal property within 3 months of P.R. appointment; P.R. must hire private appraiser.
Claims: Due within 6 months of first creditor publication.
P.R. Fees: Up to 5%.
Attorney Fees: Reasonable fee.

NEW MEXICO: District and Probate Courts
Statutes: New Mexico Statutes Annotated, 1978 (Amendments to 1985), Ch. 45 (UPC).
Administration: *Unsupervised* — For all estates except as follows. *Supervised* — Upon petition, court imposes limited or complete supervision ranging from stopping a sale to continuing control of estate. *Summary* — If estate (minus some real estate claims) totals less than spouse's automatic share and administration, funeral, last-illness costs. *By Affidavit* — Collect personal property if estate less than $20,000, inheritor applies at least 30 days after death and no P.R. application is pending.
Spouse's Automatic Share: 1/2 community property, personal property up to $3,500, living expenses up to $10,000 and, in certain cases, homestead up to $100,000.
Spouse's Intestate Share: Entire estate if no living issue; otherwise 1/4 separate property.
Spouse's Right of Election: No provision.
Proving Will: *Informal Hearing* — Testimony or affidavit of anyone with knowledge of execution. *Formal Hearing [Uncontested]* — Testimony or affidavit of 1 signing witness.

[Contested] — Testimony of 1 signing witness or other evidence. Self-proved wills accepted.
Nonresident P.R.: Yes.
Notice: *Before Proving Will [Formal Hearing]* — At least 14 days before hearing, give or mail to surviving spouse, those who could take by intestacy or will and P.R. named in any will. If address or identity unknown, publish once a week 2 consecutive weeks. *[Informal Hearing]* — Same as above except only upon request. *Before P.R. Appointment [Formal Hearing]* — Same as Before Proving Will; send also to creditors and anyone claiming same or greater right to be P.R. *[Informal Hearing]* — Same as above except only mail upon request and to anyone with same or greater right to be P.R. *After P.R. Appointment* — Within 10 days of appointment, give or mail to spouse, those who could take by intestacy or will, and others upon request. *To Creditors* — Unless already given, publish once a week 2 consecutive weeks.
Forms of Property: Community property state. Tenancy in common, joint tenancy, community property recognized. Spouses may hold real estate as joint tenants. No tenancy by entirety.
Inventory, Appraisal: Within 3 months of P.R. appointment. P.R. may hire private appraiser.
Claims: Within 2 months of first creditor notice; if no notice, within 3 years of death.
P.R. Fees: Up to 10% of first $3,000; 5% of balance excluding life insurance proceeds, cash, checking accounts, time deposits, C.D.s, savings, postal savings and U.S. bonds.
Attorney Fees: Same as P.R.

NEW YORK: Surrogate's Court
Statutes: McKinney's Consolidated Laws of New York Annotated, Surrogate's Court Procedure Act, Vol. 58A, and Estates, Powers, and Trust Law, Vol. 17B, 1981 (Amendments to 1986).
Administration: *Unsupervised* — For all estates except as follows. *Supervised*: Upon petition, at court's discretion.
Administration Unnecessary (Voluntary Administrator) — For estates with less than $10,000 in personal property (excluding spouse's automatic share) if surviving spouse applies; if no spouse, executor, if no executor, next inheritor. *By Affidavit* — At least 30 days after death, collect payment for debts up to $10,000.
Spouse's Automatic Share: Living expense and use of home for 40 days after death; household personal property up to $5,000; farm machines up to $10,000; other personal property up to $1,000 if not needed to pay funeral expenses.
Spouse's Intestate Share: 1) Entire estate if no living issue

or parent; 2) $25,000 plus 1/2 balance if living parent and no issue; 3) $4,000 and 1/2 balance if 1 child or only 1 issue of deceased child; 4) $4,000 and 1/3 balance if more than 1 issue.
Spouse's Right of Election: 1/2 estate (which includes joint property) if living issue; otherwise, 1/3 estate. Must elect within 6 months of P.R. appointment.
Proving Will: *Uncontested* —Testimony (or affidavit, at court's discretion) of at least 1 signing witness. *Contested* — Testimony of 1 signing witness. Self-proved wills accepted.
Nonresident P.R.: Yes.
Notice: *Before Proving Will* — None required if all who could take by intestacy or will consent. If all do not consent, at least 10 days before court-set date, court summons served on those who could take by intestacy or will. *Before P.R. Appointment* — Mail to those who could take by intestacy or will and who have not waived notice or appeared at hearing to prove will. *Before Administration If No Will* — Same as Before Proving Will except only to those who could take by intestacy or have same or greater right to be P.R. At court's discretion, mail to each person who has not yet received or waived notice, or appeared at hearing for P.R. appointment. *After P.R. Appointment, to Creditors* — Not required unless court directs.
Forms of Property: Tenancy in common, joint tenancy and tenancy by entirety recognized. Joint ownership by spouses presumes tenancy by entirety unless specified otherwise. Joint ownership by couples not legally married but who are described as husband and wife presumes joint tenancy unless tenancy in common stated. Tenancy by entirety in personal property not recognized.
Inventory, Appraisal: Within 6 months of proving will. P.R. may hire private appraiser.
Claims: Within 3 months of first publication; if no publication, within 7 months of P.R. appointment.
P.R. Fees: Up to 5% of all income and payments less than $100,000; 4% of next $200,000; 3% of next $700,000; 2.5% of next $4,000,000; 2% over $5,000,000. May award higher fee.
Attorney Fees: Reasonable fee.

NORTH CAROLINA: Superior Court
Statutes: General Statutes of North Carolina, 1984 (Amendments to 1985), Vol. 2A, Part I, Ch. 28-41.
Administration: *Supervised* — For all estates except as follows. *By Affidavit* — Collect personal property for estates with only personal property less than $10,000 if inheritor applies at least 30 days after death.

Spouse's Automatic Share: Living expenses between $5,000 and 1/2 annual income of deceased for 1 year at court's discretion.

Spouse's Intestate Share: 1) Entire estate if no living parents or issue; 2) $15,000 personal property plus 1/2 balance if 1 living child; 3) $15,000 personal property plus 1/3 balance if 2 or more children, or 1 child and 1 issue of deceased child, or 2 or more issue of 2 or more deceased children; 3) $25,000 personal property plus 1/2 balance if no issue but living parent. Spouse may apply for different proportions of real estate and personal property. Must apply within 7 months of P.R. appointment.

Spouse's Right of Election: Lifetime use of home or 1/3 real estate owned during marriage, whichever is greater. May elect if inherited share is less than intestate share. Must elect within 7 months of P.R. appointment.

Proving Will: *Informal Hearing (Common Form)*— Testimony of 2 signing witnesses; if 1 witness incompetent, out of state or refuses, testimony of 1 available witness and proof of handwriting of other witness and deceased; if unavailable, other evidence. Self-proved wills accepted. *Formal Hearing (Solemn Form)* —Testimony of anyone who could take by intestacy, will or claim against the estate.

Nonresident P.R.: Yes, If appoint resident agent.

Notice: *Before Proving Will, P.R. Appointment* — Court serves summons on those who could take by intestacy or will and to persons with same or greater right to be P.R. *After Proving Will, to Creditors* — Within 20 days of P.R. appointment, publish once a week 4 consecutive weeks in paper; if no paper, post at courthouse and 4 public places.

Forms of Property: Tenancy in common, joint tenancy and tenancy by entirety recognized. Tenancy by entirety in personal property not recognized.

Inventory, Appraisal: Within 3 months of P.R. appointment. P.R. may hire private appraisers.

Claims: Within six months of first creditor publication.

P.R. Fees: Up to 5% of income and payments. If estate $2,000 or less, clerk fixes fee.

Attorney Fees: Reasonable fee.

NORTH DAKOTA: District and County Courts

Statutes: North Dakota Century Code Annotated 1980 (Amendments to 1986), Title 30 (UPC).

Administration: *Unsupervised*— For all estates except as follows. *Supervised* — Upon petition, court imposes limited or complete supervision ranging from stopping a sale to continuing control of estate. *By Affidavit* — For estates less than $15,000 if 30 days after death and no P.R. application is pending. *Summary* — If estate (minus some real estate claims) totals

less than homestead, spouse's automatic share and administration, funeral, last-illness costs.
Spouse's Automatic Share: Lifetime use of house and adjoining land up to $80,000 before creditors but not other inheritors; personal property up to $5,000 and living expenses set by court.
Spouse's Intestate Share: 1) Entire estate if no living issue or parent; 2) $50,000 and 1/2 balance if living parent but no living issue, or if living issue are all surviving spouse's; 3) 1/2 estate if 1 or more living issue are not surviving spouse's.
Spouse's Right of Election: 1/3 estate (which includes certain gifts from deceased and joint property). Must elect within 9 months of death or 6 months after proving will, whichever is later.
Proving Will: *Informal Hearing* — Testimony or affidavit of anyone with knowledge of execution. *Formal Hearing [Uncontested]* — Testimony or affidavit of 1 signing witness; if unavailable, other evidence. *[Contested]* — Testimony of 1 signing witness. Self-proved wills accepted.
Nonresident P.R.: Yes.
Notice: *Before P.R. Appointment [Formal Hearing]* — At least 14 days before hearing, give or mail to spouse and those who could take by intestacy or will; if address or identity unknown, publish once a week 3 consecutive weeks, the last at least 20 days before hearing. *[Informal Hearing]* — Same as above except only upon request. *After P.R. Appointment [Formal Hearing]* — None required. *[Informal Hearing]* — Within 30 days, mail to those who could take by intestacy or will if addresses known. *To Creditors* — Upon appointment, publish notice once a week 3 consecutive weeks.
Forms of Property: Tenancy in common and joint tenancy recognized. No tenancy by entirety.
Inventory, Appraisal: Within 3 months of appointment. P.R. may hire private appraiser.
Claims: Within 3 months of first creditor notice; or if no notice, within 3 years of death.
P.R. Fees: Reasonable fee.
Attorney Fees: Reasonable fee.

OHIO: Court of Common Pleas (Probate Division)
Statutes: Page's Ohio Revised Code Annotated 1980, Title 21 (Amendments to 1986).
Administration: *Supervised* — For all estates except as follows. *Summary (Release from Administration)* — For estates less than $15,000.
Spouse's Automatic Share: Living expenses up to $5,000 deducted from inherited share; 1 year use of house.
Spouse's Intestate Share: 1) Entire estate if no living issue; 2) $30,000 plus 1/2 balance if only 1 living child or deceased

child's issue; 3) $30,000 plus 1/3 balance if 2 or more living children or their issue; 4) $10,000 plus 1/2 balance if 1 living child not surviving spouse's; 5) $10,000 plus 1/3 balance if 2 or more living children not surviving spouse's.
Spouse's Right of Election: 1/2 estate if 1 child; otherwise 1/3 estate. Must elect within 1 month of court notice or 3 months of notice if will contested.
Proving Will: Testimony or affidavit of 2 witnesses to execution; if unavailable, other evidence. Self-proved wills accepted.
Nonresident P.R.: Yes, if named in will and close relative.
Notice: *Before Proving Will* — At least 7 days before hearing, mail to surviving spouse and those who could take by intestacy or will. *After P.R. Appointment* — Within 1 month, Probate Judge publishes once a week 3 consecutive weeks; also, within 1 month, mail to spouse and those who could take by intestacy or will. *Before Summary Administration* — Publish once a week 3 consecutive weeks unless court finds unnecessary. No notice after hearing.
Forms of Property: Tenancy in common; tenancy by entirety recognized. Express provision for survivorship recognized.
Inventory, Appraisal: Within 1 month of appointment, P.R. must hire private appraiser if surviving spouse or minor children or if value of personal property is in doubt or worth more than $500.
Claims: Within 3 months of appointment, with exceptions.
P.R. Fees: Up to 4% of first $100,000, 3% of next $300,000, 2% of balance plus 1% of real estate not sold and non-probate property used in computing Ohio estate taxes.
Attorney Fees: Varies for each county by court rules. In Stark County, fee percentages range from 6% on first $10,000 to 2.5% on $400,000 and over; in Franklin County, any fee awarded if 25% of interested parties consent.

OKLAHOMA: District Court
Statutes: Oklahoma Statutes Annotated 1969 (Amendments to 1985), Title 58.
Administration: *Supervised* — For all estates except as follows. *Summary* — For estates less than $60,000.
Spouse's Automatic Share: Homestead as long as occupant; certain personal property; living expenses at court's discretion; if estate insolvent, living expenses up to 1 year.
Spouse's Intestate Share: 1) Entire estate if no living issue, parent, grandparent, or sibling; 2) all property acquired by "joint industry" during marriage plus 1/3 balance if no issue, but living parent or sibling; 3) 1/2 estate if living issue are all surviving spouse's; 4) 1/2 property acquired by "joint industry" during marriage if living issue are not spouse's, plus equal share of balance with children; 5) 1/2 estate if living grandparent but no

issue, parent or their issue.
Spouse's Right of Election: Intestate share. Must elect within 1 month of notice to elect.
Proving Will: *Uncontested* — Testimony or affidavit of 1 signing witness. *Contested* — Testimony of all signing witnesses; if unavailable, affidavit of signing and other witnesses. Self-proved wills accepted.
Nonresident P.R.: Yes, if appoint resident agent.
Notice: *Before P.R. Appointment* — At least 10 days before hearing, mail to all who could take by intestacy or will; if name or address unknown, publish in county newspaper; if unavailable, post in 2 public places and courthouse.
Forms of Property: Tenancy in common, joint tenancy recognized. Tenancy by entirety not recognized but survivorship if stated.
Inventory, Appraisal: Within 2 months. Court may require court-appointed appraiser.
Claims: Within 2 months of first notice; if 5 years after death, within 1 month, with exceptions.
P.R. Fees: Up to 5% of first $1,000; 4% of next $4,000; 2.5% of balance.
Attorney Fees: Reasonable fee.

OREGON: Circuit and County Courts
Statutes: Oregon Revised Statutes 1985, Title 12.
Administration: *Supervised* — For all estates except as follows. *Summary* — For estates which court determines are necessary to support spouse and children after claims, taxes, expenses. *Administration Unnecessary* — For estates with personal property less than $15,000 and real estate less than $35,000 if inheritor applies at least 30 days after death.
Spouse's Automatic Share: Living expenses up to 2 years at court's discretion and use of family home for 1 year.
Spouse's Intestate Share: Entire estate after debts if no issue; otherwise 1/2 estate.
Spouse's Right of Election: 1/4 estate (after gifts and inherited share under will up to 1/2 estate). Cannot elect if waived in writing. Must elect within 90 days after proving will or 30 days after filing inventory, whichever is later.
Proving Will: *Uncontested* — Testimony or affidavit of 1 signing witness. *Contested* — Testimony of 1 signing witness, if unavailable, by affidavit or other evidence. Self-proved wills accepted.
Nonresident P.R.: Yes.
Notice: *After P.R. Appointment* — Within 30 days, give to those who could take by intestacy or will. Publish once a week 3 consecutive weeks.
Forms of Property: Tenancy in common, tenancy by entirety

recognized. Right of survivorship is stated in agreement. No tenancy by entirety for personal property.
Inventory, Appraisal: Within 60 days of P.R. appointment. P.R. may hire private appraiser.
Claims: Within 4 months after first published notice or before final accounting, whichever is earlier; if no notice, 3 years after death.
P.R. Fees: Up to 7% of first $1,000; 4% of next $9,000; 3% of next $40,000; 2% above $50,000, plus 1% of taxable Oregon property excluding life insurance.
Attorney Fees: Reasonable fee.

PENNSYLVANIA: Common Pleas Court (Orphan's Court Division) and Registrar of Wills
Statutes: Purdon's Pennsylvania Statutes Annotated 1982 (Amendments to 1986), Title 20, Decedents Estates and Fiduciaries.
Administration: *Supervised* — For all estates except as follows. *Unsupervised* — If all who could take by intestacy or will consent. *Administration Unnecessary* — For estates with only real estate plus less than $10,000 in personal property.
Spouse's Automatic Share: Living expenses up to $2,000.
Spouse's Intestate Share: 1) Entire estate if no living parent or issue; 2) $30,000 plus 1/2 balance if living issue are all surviving spouse's; 3) 1/2 balance if 1 or more living issue not surviving spouse's.
Spouse's Right of Election: 1/3 estate (which includes all property given by deceased to the spouse and any gifts over $3,000 given by deceased to anyone other than the spouse within 1 year of death). Must elect within 6 months of proving will.
Proving Will: Testimony of 2 signing witnesses or competent persons; if dead or can't remember, by proving signature or deceased or signing witnesses. Self-proved wills accepted.
Nonresident P.R.: Yes, but Registrar must approve and must appoint resident agent.
Notice: *Before P.R. Appointment* — Court may publish. *After P.R. Appointment* — Publish once a week 3 consecutive weeks in newspaper and local legal periodical.
Forms of Property: Tenancy in common and tenancy by entirety recognized. Joint tenancy with right of survivorship only if stated. Real estate jointly owned by spouses presumes tenancy by entirety unless stated otherwise. Tenancy by entirety in personal property recognized.
Inventory, Appraisal: 9 months after P.R. appointment unless requested earlier. P.R. may hire private appraiser.
Claims: Within 1 year of death.
P.R. Fees: Reasonable fee, usually up to 5% of first $100,000; 4% of next $100,000; 3% of next $800,000; 2% of next

$1,000,000; 1.5% of next $1,000,000; 1% of next $1,000,000; .5% of next $1,000,000; plus 3% of all real estate sold, 5% of other real estate and 1% of joint accounts and trust funds.
Attorney Fees: Reasonable fee up to 7% of first $25,000; 6% of next $25,000; 5% of next $50,000; 4% of next $100,000; 3% of next $900,000; 2% of next $1,000,000; 1.5 % of next $1,000,000; 1% of next $1,000,000; .5% of next $1,000,000 plus 3.5% for transferring joint accounts; 1% of assets outside will up to $1,000,000, and .5% required commission on joint accounts and trust funds.

PUERTO RICO: Superior Court
Statutes: Laws of Puerto Rico Annotated 1968 (Amendments to 1985), Code of Civil Procedures, Titles 31-32.
Administration: *Administration Unnecessary (Acceptance Without Administration)* — For all estates except as follows. *Supervised (Judicial)* — If court determines necessary or possible inheritor is under 18 or not in Puerto Rico.
Spouse's Automatic Share: 1/2 community property and 1/4 separate property.
Spouse's Intestate Share: 1) Entire estate if no living issue, parent, grandparent, great-grandparent, sibling or their issue; 2) lifetime use of property equal to child's share if living issue; 3) lifetime use of 1/2 estate if no living issue, parent or grandparent.
Spouse's Right of Election: No provision.
Proving Will: Testimony or notary and witnesses; if dead or unavailable, testimony of 2 persons proving their signatures.
Nonresident P.R.: Yes, if handle work in Puerto Rico.
Notice: *After Proving Will, to Creditors* — Publish as directed by court, usually once a week for 2 months.
Forms of Property: Community property jurisdiction. Co-ownership, community or conjugal property recognized. Property acquired during marriage belongs in equal parts to both spouses; property presumed to belong to marriage. Each spouse may dispose of 1/2 community property by will.
Inventory, Appraisal: Only if requested by inheritor; if inheritor accepts share without inventory and appraisal, inheritor is responsible for all estate debts, not only claims on inherited share.
Claims: Within 6 months of first publication.
P.R. Fees: Up to 5% of first $1,000, 2.5% of next $9,000, 1% of balance.
Attorney Fees: No provision.
Note: Upon death, some relatives inherit property automatically and can only reject personal liability for debts of the deceased by rejecting the inheritance.

RHODE ISLAND: Probate Court
Statutes: General Laws of Rhode Island 1984 (Amendments to 1985), Vol. 6, Title 33.
Administration: *Supervised* — For all estates except as follows. *Administration Unnecessary* — For estates less than $10,000 (after certain personal property) if spouse applies within 45 days after death and no P.R. application is pending.
Spouse's Automatic Share: Certain personal property and living expenses for 6 months.
Spouse's Intestate Share: $25,000 in real estate at court's discretion and lifetime use of real estate (after some real estate claims), $50,000 in personal property plus 1/2 balance if no living issue, otherwise, 1/2 personal property. Must apply within 6 months of first P.R. publication.
Spouse's Right of Election: Lifetime use of real estate (after some real estate claims) owned at death. Must elect within 6 months of proving will.
Nonresident P.R.: Yes, if appoint resident agent.
Notice: *Before Proving Will* — At least 10 days before hearing (30 days if outside U.S.), mail to those who could take by intestacy or will and to any P.R. in will who has not applied to be P.R. May also publish. *Before P.R. Appointment* — Same as above except mail at least 7 days before hearing. *After P.R. Appointment, to Creditors* — Published by clerk as court directs.
Forms of Property: Tenancy in common, joint tenancy and tenancy by entirety recognized.
Inventory, Appraisal: Within 30 days of appointment with exceptions. Upon request, court may appoint appraisers.
Claims: Within 6 months of published notice.
P.R. Fees: Reasonable fee.
Attorney Fees: Reasonable fee.

SOUTH CAROLINA: Probate Court
Statutes: Codes of South Carolina 1976 (Amendments to 1985), Vol. 9, Title 21.
Administration: *Supervised* — For all estates except as follows. *Summary* — For intestate estates with less than $7,500 in personal property.
Spouse's Intestate Share: 1) 1/3 estate if more than 1 living child; 2) 1/2 estate if only 1 living child, or no child but grandparent, parent, sibling, niece or nephew; 3) entire estate if none of the above.
Spouse's Automatic Share: No provision.
Spouse's Right of Election: No provision.
Proving Will: *Informal Hearing (Common Form)* —

Testimony of 1 signing witness; if dead, testimony proving handwriting of deceased and 1 signing witness; if unavailable, other evidence. **Formal Hearing (Solemn Form)** — Testimony of all signing witnesses; if unavailable, other evidence.
Nonresident P.R.: Yes, if appoint resident agent.
Notice: *Before P.R. Appointment* — If no will, judge posts on courthouse door for 2 weeks and (in some counties) publishes in newspaper. *After P.R. Appointment, to Creditors* — Within 30 days of appointment, publish in newspaper once a week for 3 weeks.
Forms of Property: Tenancy in common and joint tenancy recognized. Right of survivorship only if stated. No tenancy by entirety.
Inventory, Appraisal: Inventory due within 1 month after P.R. appointment; appraisal due within 1 month of inventory. P.R. must hire court-appointed appraiser.
Claims: Within 5 months after first publication.
P.R. Fees: Up to 5% of appraised value of personal property more than $50; 10% of profit on investments.
Attorney Fees: No provision.
Note: Recent revisions in probate code not reflected above will take effect July 1987. Ask court clerk.

SOUTH DAKOTA: Circuit Court
Statutes: South Dakota Codified Laws 1984 (Amendments to 1986), Vol. 19B, Ch. 29, 30.
Administration: *Unsupervised (Independent)* — For all estates except as follows. *Supervised* — Upon petition, court imposes limited or complete supervision ranging from stopping a sale to continuing control of estate. *Summary* — For estates less than $60,000 if any inheritor applies with estimated inventory.
Spouse's Automatic Share: Lifetime use of homestead before creditors, personal property up to $1,500, and living expenses during administration; if insolvent, living expenses for only 1 year.
Spouse's Intestate Share: 1) Entire estate if no living issue, parent, sibling or their issue; 2) 1/2 estate if only 1 living issue; 3) 1/3 estate if 1 living child and issue of deceased child, or living issue of 2 or more deceased children; 4) $100,000 and 1/2 balance or elective share if no living issue but living parent, sibling or their issue.
Spouse's Right of Election: $100,000 or 1/3 property in will, whichever is greater. Must elect within 2 months of first creditor notice.
Proving Will: *Uncontested* — None if copies of properly witnessed will mailed to those who could take by intestacy or will.
Contested —Testimony of all signing witnesses in county; if not

in county or physically unable to testify, by affidavit.
Nonresident P.R.: Yes, if appoint resident agent.
Notice: *Before P.R. Appointment, Proving Will* — At least 14 days before hearing, mail judge-approved notice to those who could take by intestacy or will. *To Creditors* — Publish once a week 3 consecutive weeks, the last at least 15 days before hearing to prove will.
Forms of Property: Tenancy in common and joint tenancy recognized. No tenancy by entirety. Creditors' rights preserved against surviving joint owners.
Inventory, Appraisal: Within 9 months of death. P.R. may hire private appraiser.
Claims: Due within 2 months of first publication.
P.R. Fees: Up to 5% of first $1,000 of personal property and real estate sold; 4% of next $4,000; 2.5% of amounts over $5,000, and fee for real estate not sold.
Attorney Fees: No provision.

TENNESSEE: Chancery Court (Probate Court in Davidson and Shelby Counties)
Statutes: Tennessee Code Annotated 1984 (Amendments to 1986), Vol. 6, 3-101 to 32-5110.
Administration: *Supervised* — For all estates except as follows. *Summary* — For estates with only personal property less than $10,000 if inheritor by intestacy or will applies at least 45 days after death.
Spouse's Automatic Share: Lifetime use of homestead up to $5,000 and living expenses based on standard of living for previous year; may take personal property instead of money.
Spouse's Intestate Share: 1) Entire estate if no living issue; 2) 1/2 estate if only 1 living issue; 3) 1/3 estate or child's share, whichever is greater, if more than 1 living issue.
Spouse's Right of Election: 1/3 real estate. Must elect within 9 months after death or 6 months after proving will, whichever is later.
Proving Will: *Informal Hearing (Common Form)* — Affidavit or testimony of at least 1 signing witness. *Formal Hearing (Solemn Form)* — All signing witnesses and others with information about will's validity may testify; if unavailable, testimony of at least 1 signing witness proving signature of deceased.
Nonresident P.R.: Yes, if appoint resident co-P.R.
Notice: *Before Proving Will [Informal Hearing (Common Form)]*— None required. *[Formal Hearing (Solemn Form)]* — 30 days before hearing, mail or give court order to anyone who could take by intestacy or will. *After P.R. Appointment, to Creditors*: Within 30 days of appointment, clerk publishes

Appendix I

consecutive weeks in county newspaper; if no newspaper, clerk posts in 3 public places and courthouse. If estate less than $1,000, post only.
Forms of Property: Tenancy in common and tenancy by entirety recognized. Survivorship in joint tenancy created only if stated in ownership document.
Inventory, Appraisal: Within 60 days of P.R. appointment. P.R. may hire private appraiser.
Claims: Within 6 months of first publication.
P.R. Fees: Reasonable fee.
Attorney Fees: Reasonable fee; in practice 3-5% of estate.

TEXAS: County or Statutory Probate Court
Statutes: Vernon's Civil Statutes of the State of Texas Annotated 1980 (Amendments to 1986), Probate Code, Vol. 17.
Administration: *Unsupervised (Independent)* — For all estates if those who could take by intestacy or will consent. *Supervised (Dependent)* — If P.R. fails to return inventory and accounting on time or grossly mismanages estate, upon petition, court will take continuing control. **Administration Unnecessary** — 1) For estates with only less than $50,000 personal property (after spouse's automatic share) if inheritor applies at least 30 days after death; 2) for estates (after homestead and personal property) less than spouse's living expenses if spouse applies; 3) if inheritor posts bond double the appraised value.
Spouse's Automatic Share: 1/2 community property plus certain personal property or $1,000 and, at court's discretion, lifetime use of home and 1 acre in city, 200 acres outside; living expenses for 1 year. If no home, $10,000.
Spouse's Right of Election: No provision.
Spouse's Intestate Share: *Community Property* — All if no living issue, otherwise none. *Separate Property* — 1) All if no living issue, parent, sibling or their issue; 2) 1/3 personal property and lifetime use of real estate if living issue; 3) 1/2 estate if no living issue but parent, sibling, or their issue. Spouse must elect before hearing to prove will.
Proving Will: Testimony or affidavit of 1 signing witness; if not a county resident or unable to attend and will uncontested, affidavit; if witnesses are dead or in armed forces out of court's jurisdiction, 2 witnesses proving handwriting of deceased and signing witnesses. Self-proved wills accepted.
Nonresident P.R.: Yes, if appoint resident agent.
Notice: *Before Proving Will, P.R. Appointment* — 10 days before hearing, clerk posts in courthouse. *After P.R. Appointment, to Creditors* — Within 1 month, publish in county newspaper, send to Comptroller of Public Accounts if

taxes owed or paid, and (except in Unsupervised Administration) within 4 months, send by registered mail to anyone who has notified P.R. or court of a claim.
Forms of Property: Community property state. All property acquired by either spouse during marriage is community property. Tenancy in common recognized. No tenancy by entirety.
Inventory, Appraisal: Within 90 days. Court appoints 1 to 3 appraisers.
Claims: Within 6 months of P.R. appointment.
P.R. Fees: Up to 5% of ingoing and outgoing cash; not allowed for cash on hand at death or money distributed to inheritors. Court may award higher fee.
Attorney Fees: Reasonable fee.

UTAH: District Court
Statutes: Utah Code Annotated 1978 (Amendments to 1986), Probate Code, Vol. 8A.
Administration: *Unsupervised* — For all estates except as follows. *Supervised* — Upon petition, the court imposes limited or complete supervision ranging from stopping a sale to continuing control of estate. *Summary* — If estate (minus some real estate claims) totals less than spouse's automatic share plus administration, funeral and last illness costs.
Spouse's Automatic Share: Living expenses during administration up to 1 year, 4 vehicles up to $25,000, certain personal property up to $3,500, and home up to $6,000.
Spouse's Intestate Share: 1) Entire estate if no living issue or parent; 2) $100,000 plus 1/2 balance if no living issue but parent; 3) $50,000 plus 1/2 balance if living issue are all surviving spouse's; 4) 1/2 estate if 1 or more living issue are not surviving spouse's.
Spouse's Right of Election: 1/3 estate (which includes certain property given by deceased to spouse). If elect within 6 months, estate includes assets not in will. Must elect within 1 year.
Proving Will: *Informal Hearing* — None required if will is properly executed; otherwise, testimony or affidavit of anyone with knowledge of execution. Formal Hearing Uncontested — Testimony or affidavit of 1 signing witness; if unavailable, other evidence. *Contested* — Testimony of at least 1 signing witness; if out-of-state or incompetent, other evidence. Self-proved wills accepted.
Nonresident P.R.: Yes.
Notice: *Before Proving Will [Formal Hearing]* — Clerk posts at least 10 consecutive days in 2 public places and in courthouse immediately before hearing. At least 10 days before hearing, clerk

mails to spouse, children and P.R. named in any will offered for probate; if address or identity unknown, clerk publishes once a week 3 consecutive weeks. *[Informal Hearing]* — Same as Before Formal Hearing except clerk mails only to those who could take by intestacy or will. **Before P.R. Appointment** *[Formal Hearing]* — Same as Before Proving Will except clerk mails also to anyone who claims same or greater right to be P.R. *[Informal Hearing]* — Same as Before Proving Will except clerk mails only to those who could take by intestacy or will. **After P.R. Appointment, to Creditors** — Unless already given, promptly publish once a week 3 consecutive weeks. **Summary Administration** — None required.
Forms of Property: Tenancy in common, joint tenancy and tenancy by entirety recognized. Joint tenancy only if stated.
Inventory, Appraisal: Within 3 months of P.R. appointment. P.R. may hire private appraiser.
Claims: Within 3 months of first publication, if no notice, within 3 years of death.
P.R. Fees: Up to 5% of first $1,000; 4% of next $4,000; 3% of next $5,000; 2% of next $40,000; 1.5% of next $50,000; 1% over $100,000.
Attorney Fees: Up to 5% of first $20,000; 4% of next $40,000; 3% of next $140,000; 2.5% of next $550,000; 2% of next $750,000; 1% of balance.

VERMONT: Probate Court
Statutes: Vermont Statutes Annotated 1974 (Amendments to 1986), Title 14; Rules of Probate Procedure 1986.
Administration: *Supervised* — For all estates except as follows. *Summary* — For all estates with only less than $10,000 in personal property if surviving spouse or adult children apply. *Administration Unnecessary* — Court may give estates less than $300 to spouse.
Spouse's Automatic Share: Homestead up to $30,000, plus living expenses through administration, if estate insolvent, up to 8 months.
Spouse's Intestate Share: 1) $25,000 and 1/2 balance if no living issue; 2) 1/3 personal property and 1/2 real estate if only 1 living issue and issue is also surviving spouse's; 3) 1/3 personal property and 1/3 real estate if 2 or more living issue or 1 or more living issue is not surviving spouse's.
Spouse's Right of Election: If only 1 living issue and issue is spouse's, 1/2 real estate owned at death, after debts; otherwise 1/3. Must elect within 8 months of proving will.
Proving Will: If those who could take by intestacy consent, will accepted without further evidence; otherwise, testimony of 1 signing witness; if out-of-state, in armed forces or physically or

mentally ill, testimony of 2 witnesses proving sanity and handwriting of deceased and proper execution of will.
Nonresident P.R.: Yes, if surviving spouse; if none, adult children; if none, parent applies and P.R. appoints resident agent; otherwise, at court's discretion.
Notice: *Before P.R. Appointment, Proving Will*— At least 14 days before hearing, P.R. or court (if no lawyer) mails to surviving spouse, children, and those who could take by intestacy or will; if address unknown, publish once a week 2 consecutive weeks. *After P.R. Appointment, to Creditors* — Within 30 days, publish twice at least 7 days apart. For estates less than $2,500 and estates with debts arranged or paid, no creditor notice necessary. Also, court mails to those named in will or who could take by intestacy.
Forms of Property: Tenancy in common, joint tenancy and tenancy by entirety recognized.
Inventory, Appraisal: Within 30 days. P.R. may hire private appraiser.
Claims: Within 4 months of first creditor notice; if no notice, within 3 years of death.
P.R. Fees: Reasonable fee.
Attorney Fees: Reasonable fee.

VIRGIN ISLANDS: Territorial and District Court
Statutes: Virgin Islands Code Annotated 1965 (Amendments to 1985), Vol. 3, Title 15, Vol. 2, Probate and Fiduciary Rules Appendix.
Administration: *Supervised*— For all estates except as follows. *Summary* — For estates less than $300. *Administration Unnecessary (Settlement Without Administration)*— For solvent intestate estates if inheritors consent and accept debts on inherited share. *By Affidavit*— Collect payment for debts less than $1,000. Adult children, parent or sibling may apply if 30 days after death. Spouse may apply anytime.
Spouse's Automatic Share: Use of home and clothing until inventory; thereafter court sets aside property deemed necessary for support. Additional support if P.R. requests and court orders.
Spouse's Intestate Share: 1) 1/3 estate if living issue; 2) $5,000 and 1/2 balance if living parent but no issue; 3) $10,000 and 1/2 balance if living sibling or their children, but no living issue or parent; 4) otherwise, entire estate.
Spouse's Right of Election: Intestate share up to 1/2 estate (after debts, estate taxes and funeral and administration costs). Must elect within 6 months of P.R. appointment.
Proving Will: Testimony or affidavits of signing witnesses, or other evidence.

Nonresident P.R.: If named in will and appoint resident agent.
Notice: *Before Proving Will*— Unless waived, give or (outside islands) mail as court orders to those who could take by intestacy or will. If addresses unknown, publish 3 consecutive weeks, the first 20 days before hearing date. *After P.R. Appointment, to Creditors*— Promptly publish once a week 4 consecutive weeks; post in post office and 2 public places chosen by court. *Summary Administration*— If estate less than $200, only post for 2 weeks.
Forms of Property: Tenancy in common, joint tenancy and tenancy by entirety recognized. Joint ownership by spouses presumes tenancy by entirety unless stated otherwise.
Inventory, Appraisal: Within 1 month of P.R. appointment. P.R. must hire court-appointed appraiser.
Claims: Within 6 months of first creditor notice. In Summary Administration due within 30 days of first creditor notice.
P.R. Fees: Reasonable fee.
Attorney Fees: No provision.

VIRGINIA: Circuit Court
Statutes: Code of Virginia 1980 (Amendments to 1986), Vol. 9A, Titles 63.1-65.1.
Administration: *Supervised*— For all estates except as follows. *By Affidavit*— If inheritor applies at least 60 days after death, and no P.R. application is pending, collect personal property for estates less than $5,000.
Spouse's Automatic Share: Personal property up to $3,500; home up to $5,000 (deducted from inherited share); living expenses during administration, 1 year if estate insolvent.
Spouse's Intestate Share: 1/3 estate if 1 or more living issue not surviving spouse's; otherwise, entire estate.
Spouse's Right of Election: 1/3 estate if living issue; otherwise, 1/2. Must elect within 1 year of proving will.
Proving Will: *Informal Hearing (Ex Parte)* — Testimony of 1 signing witness; if unavailable, testimony proving witness signatures, if unavailable, court presumes valid. *Formal Hearing (Inter Partes)* — All possible inheritors may testify. Self-proved wills accepted.
Nonresident P.R.: No, unless P.R. is sole inheritor and appoints resident agent; otherwise, must serve with resident.
Notice: *After P.R. Appointment* — Within 20 days, give to those who could take by intestacy or will. *To Creditors*— Publish once a week 4 consecutive weeks with last publication at least 2 weeks before closing.
Forms of Property: Tenancy in common, joint tenancy and tenancy by entirety recognized. Joint tenancy with right of survivorship created if stated.
Inventory, Appraisal: Within 4 months of P.R. appointment

for estate over $500. P.R. may hire private appraiser subject to court approval.
Claims: Within 1 year of creditor notice or at hearing for "creditors to show cause," which P.R. may request 6 months after appointment.
P.R. Fees: Reasonable fee; in practice, usually 5%.
Attorney Fees: No provision.
Note: Virginia requires a Commissioner of Accounts to review the final inventory and accounting. Ask circuit clerk for commissioner fee schedule and probate information.

WASHINGTON: Superior Court (Probate Division)
Statutes: Revised Code of Washington 1967 (Amendments to 1986), Title 11.
Administration: *Unsupervised (Without Intervention of Court)* — For all solvent estates if P.R. is not a creditor. *Supervised* — If requested in will, estate is insolvent or upon petition, the court may restrict powers of P.R. *By Affidavit* — Collect personal property if apply at least 40 days after death, no P.R. application is pending and solvent estate less than $10,000 (after surviving spouse's community property and certain real estate claims).
Spouse's Automatic Share: 1/2 community property, reasonable living expenses during administration, plus, at court's discretion, home and other property up to $25,000 after payment of debts and last-illness, funeral and administrative costs.
Spouse's Intestate Share: 1) Entire estate if no living issue, parent or parent's issue; 2) all community property and 3/4 separate property if no living issue but parent or parent's issue; 3) all community property and 1/2 separate property if living issue.
Spouse's Right of Election: No provision.
Proving Will: Testimony of 2 signing witnesses; if ill, out-of-state or 30 or more miles from hearing, may give testimony to an authorized person; otherwise, by proof of handwriting or deceased and witnesses or other evidence.
Nonresident P.R.: Yes, if appoint resident agent.
Notice: *After P.R. Appointment, to Creditors* — Publish in county newspaper 3 consecutive weeks, file copy with court and within 20 days, give or mail to those who could take by intestacy or will if address known. *By Affidavit (Special)* — Mail to all other inheritors 10 days before collecting property.
Forms of Property: Community property state. Tenancy in common, joint tenancy recognized. Joint tenancy with right of survivorship created if stated. No survivorship rights in tenancy by entirety. Property acquired during marriage is community

property. Surviving spouse is entitled to all community property if deceased did not otherwise dispose of it by will.
Inventory, Appraisal: Within 3 months of appointment. P.R. may hire private appraiser.
Claims: Within 4 months of first publication or of filing copy with clerk, whichever is later.
P.R. Fees: Reasonable fee subject to consent of inheritors or court approval.
Attorney Fees: No statutory provision.

WEST VIRGINIA: County Commission
Statutes: West Virginia Code 1982 (Amendments to 1986), Vol. 12, Ch. 41-44.
Administration: *Supervised* — For all estates except as follows. *Summary* — For all estates with only 1 inheritor; for insolvent estates less than $50,000 and solvent estates less than $100,000 in Braxton, Kanawha, Marion, Putnam and Summers counties.
Spouse's Automatic Share: Personal property up to $1,000 and use of family home until children are 21 or dower share taken.
Spouse's Intestate Share: Entire estate if no living issue; otherwise, 1/3 estate.
Spouse's Right of Election: 1/3 estate. Instead, may elect lifetime use of 1/3 real estate dower. Must elect within 8 months of proving will.
Proving Will: *Informal Hearing (Common Form)* — Testimony of signing witnesses; if unavailable, by proving signature of deceased or witnesses, or other evidence. *Formal Hearing (Solemn Form)* — Same as above. Self-proved wills accepted.
Nonresident P.R.: Only if parent, sibling, child, grandchild or sole inheritor. Nonresident P.R. must appoint County Commissioner as service agent and post bond.
Notice: *After P.R. Appointment, to Creditors* — Fiduciary Supervisor or Commissioner publishes notice. *Summary Administration* — County clerk publishes once a week 2 consecutive weeks before final accounting.
Forms of Property: Tenancy in common, joint tenancy recognized but right of survivorship created if stated.
Inventory, Appraisal: Within 8 months of P.R. appointment. County Commission appoints 3 to 5 appraisers.
Claims: Within 2-3 months after notice published by P.R. In Summary Administration, at final accounting.
P.R. Fees: Reasonable fee.
Attorney Fees: Reasonable fee.

Note: A Fiduciary Commissioner or Fiduciary Supervisor usually supervises inventory and accounting and reviews Summary probates. Fiduciary fees: up to $200.

WISCONSIN: Circuit Court
Statutes: Wisconsin Statutes Annotated 1971 (Amendments to 1986), Vol. 40, Sec. 851-879.
Administration: *Unsupervised (Informal Hearing)* — If requested in will or all inheritors consent. *Supervised (Formal Hearing)* — Upon petition, court imposes limited or complete supervision ranging from stopping a sale to continuing control of estate. *Summary* — For estates less than $10,000 if spouse applies; less than $5,000 if no living spouse, and sole inheritor applies. *By Affidavit* — Collect up to $5,000 of separate property plus up to 5 motor vehicles if surviving spouse applies to Division of Motor Vehicles.
Spouse's Automatic Share: 1/2 property acquired during marriage after January 1, 1986; 1/2 property on which money was spent or earned after January 1, 1986; personal property up to $1,000 and, at court's discretion, lifetime use or full ownership of home up to $10,000 plus living expenses during administration.
Spouse's Intestate Share: 1) Entire estate if no living issue or if living issue are all spouse's; 2) 1/2 estate if 1 or more living issue are not surviving spouse's.
Spouse's Right of Election: No provision.
Proving Will: *Uncontested* — None required if will properly executed. *Contested* — Testimony of 1 signing witness; if out-of-state or absence explained, affidavit; if unavailable, testimony proving handwriting of other witness and deceased.
Nonresident P.R.: Yes, if appoint resident agent.
Notice: *Before P.R. Appointment, Proving Will* — Unless waived, mail at least 20 days (or give at least 10 days) before hearing to those who could take by intestacy or will. Publish once a week 3 consecutive weeks. *After P.R. Appointment, Unsupervised Administration* — Mail within 10 days to all who could take by intestacy or will. *After Proving Will, to Creditors* — Publish 3 times, beginning within 15 days of registrar ordering claims due. *Summary (No Spouse)* — Publish once after applying for administration.
Forms of Property: Tenancy in common, joint tenancy recognized. Ownership by spouses presumes joint tenancy unless document states otherwise. No tenancy by entirety.
Inventory, Appraisal: Within 6 months of appointment. P.R. may hire private appraiser; in Supervised Administration, court may appoint appraiser if property value in reasonable doubt.

Claims: Within 3 months of court order. In Summary Administration within 30 days of publication if no spouse.
P.R. Fees: Up to 2% of all property after some claims.
Attorney Fees: Reasonable fee.

WYOMING: District Court

Statutes: Wyoming Statutes Annotated 1970 (Amendments to 1986), Vol. 2, Title 2.
Administration: *Supervised* — For all estates except as follows. *Administration Unnecessary* — For estates less than $30,000 if inheritor applies 30 days after death and no P.R. application is pending or if P.R. is sole inheritor after debts.
Spouse's Automatic Share: Use of home and clothing until inventory; reasonable living expenses at court's discretion; in certain cases, family home up to $30,000.
Spouse's Intestate Share: Entire estate if no living issue; otherwise, 1/2 estate.
Spouse's Right of Election: 1/2 estate if no living issue or living issue are all spouse's; 1/4 estate if 1 or more living issue are not surviving spouse's. Must elect within 3 months of proving will or 30 days after notice, whichever is later.
Proving Will: Testimony or affidavit of 1 signing witness; if dead or unavailable, testimony of 2 witnesses proving handwriting of deceased and witnesses. Self-proved wills accepted.
Nonresident P.R.: Yes, if named in will and appoint resident agent; if no will, must serve with resident.
Notice: *After P.R. Appointment* — Publish once a week 3 consecutive weeks. *To Creditors* — Combined with above.
Forms of Property: Tenancy in common, joint tenancy and tenancy by entirety recognized.
Inventory, Appraisal: Within 120 days. P.R. may hire private appraiser.
Claims: Within 3 months of first publication.
P.R. Fees: Up to 10% of first $1,000; 5% of next $4,000; 3% of next $15,000; 2% of $20,000.
Attorney Fees: No provision; usually same as P.R. fees.

Appendix II

STATE TAXES

Every state except Nevada imposes one or more of three types of tax on the transfer of the property of a deceased person. The three types — inheritance tax, estate tax and the credit estate tax — are discussed in detail in Chapter 9,*"Taxes."*

The tax rates listed below indicate the minimum and maximum percentages that are assessed in each state. The rate that applies to each specific case within a state depends on several factors: 1) the relationship of the heir to the deceased person, 2) the size of the total estate, and 3) the share distributed to a particular person.

For example, in Connecticut a spouse of a deceased person would not be taxed on the first $100,000 inherited, but would have to pay 2 percent on any inheritance valued at more than $100,000. The percentage would increase as the value of the inheritance increased. The exemptions are calculated after all claims, funeral costs, estate administration expenses and other allowable deductions are subtracted.

The category *Credit Estate Tax* applies only to estates that owe federal estate taxes. (See page 52 to determine whether your estate qualifies.) The tax is equal to the maximum federal credit the federal government allows for payment of state inheritance and estate taxes. The specific tax rate in your state depends on the value of the estate after subtracting all deductions, exemptions and other credits.

Because tax rates and exemption levels may change at any time, it is advisable to check the accuracy of the information for your state with your state department of revenue and taxation.

ALABAMA
Inheritance Tax: None.
Estate Tax: None.
Credit Estate Tax: Yes.
Special Provisions: None.

ALASKA
Inheritance Tax: None.
Estate Tax: None.
Credit Estate Tax: Yes.
Special Provisions: None.

ARIZONA
Inheritance Tax: None.
Estate Tax: None.
Credit Estate Tax: Yes.
Special Provisions: None.

ARKANSAS
Inheritance Tax: None.
Estate Tax: None.
Credit Estate Tax: Yes.
Special Provisions: None.

CALIFORNIA
Inheritance Tax: None. Repealed for estates of persons dying after June 9, 1982.
Estate Tax: None.
Credit Estate Tax: Yes.
Special Provisions: None.

COLORADO
Inheritance Tax: None.
Estate Tax: None.
Credit Estate Tax: Yes.
Special Provisions: None.

CONNECTICUT
Inheritance Tax: Inheriting spouse, child or parent pays 2-8 percent; brother or sister pays 4-10 percent; all others pay 8-14 percent.
Property exempt from taxation: $100,000 for spouse; $20,000 for child or parent; $6,000 for brother or sister; $1,000 for all others.
Estate Tax: None.
Credit Estate Tax: Yes.
Special Provisions: A 30 percent surtax is added to all inheritance taxes, plus 10 percent for estates of persons who died on or after July 1, 1983; this additional 10 percent is not assessed against

farmland that is transferred to natural or adopted descendants of the deceased person.

DELAWARE
Inheritance Tax: Inheriting spouse, child or parent pays 1-6 percent; brother or sister pays 5-10 percent; all others pay 10-16 percent.
Property exempt from taxation: $70,000 for spouse; $3,000 for child or parent; $1,000 for brother or sister; none for all others.
Estate Tax: None.
Credit Estate Tax: Yes.
Special Provisions: None.

DISTRICT OF COLUMBIA
Inheritance Tax: Inheriting spouse, child or parent pays 1- 8 percent; all others pay 5-23 percent. Property exempt from taxation: $5,000 for spouse, child or parent; $1,000 for all others.
Estate Tax: None.
Credit Estate Tax: Yes.
Special Provisions: None.

FLORIDA
Inheritance Tax: None.
Estate Tax: None.
Credit Estate Tax: Yes.
Special Provisions: None.

GEORGIA
Inheritance Tax: None.
Estate Tax: None.
Credit Estate Tax: Yes.
Special Provisions: None.

HAWAII
Inheritance Tax: None. Repealed for estates of persons dying after June 30, 1983.
Estate Tax: None.
Credit Estate Tax: Yes.
Special Provisions: None.

IDAHO
Inheritance Tax: Inheriting spouse, child or parent pays 2-15 percent; brother or sister pays 4-20 percent; all others pay 6-30 percent.

Property exempt from taxation: $50,000 for spouse or minor child; $30,000 for parent and other children; $10,000 for all others.
Estate Tax: None.
Credit Estate Tax: Yes.
Special Provisions: None.

ILLINOIS

Inheritance Tax: None. Repealed for estates of persons dying after
December 31, 1982.
Estate Tax: None.
Credit Estate Tax: Yes.
Special Provisions: None.

INDIANA

Inheritance Tax: Inheriting spouse, child or parent pays 1-10 percent; brother or sister pays 7-15 percent; all others pay 10-20 percent.
Property exempt from taxation: All for spouse; $10,000 for minor child; $5,000 for parent and other children; $500 for all others.
Estate Tax: None.
Credit Estate Tax: Yes.
Special Provisions: None.

IOWA

Inheritance Tax: Inheriting spouse, child or parent pays 1-8 percent; brother or sister pays 5-10 percent; all others pay 10-15 percent.
Property exempt from taxation: $180,000 for spouse; $50,000 for child; $15,000 for parent or grandchild; none for all others.
Estate Tax: None.
Credit Estate Tax: Yes.
Special Provisions: The spouse will receive a credit of one-third of the tax due on the estate of any person dying after January 1, 1986, increasing to two-thirds for the estates of persons dying after January 1, 1987. No tax on estates inherited by spouses of persons dying after January 1, 1988.

KANSAS

Inheritance Tax: Inheriting spouse, child or parent pays 1-5 percent; brother or sister pays 3-12.5 percent; all others pay 10-15 percent.
Property exempt from taxation: All for spouse; $30,000 for child or parent; $5,000 for brother or sister; none for all others.
Estate Tax: None.

Credit Estate Tax: Yes.
Special Provisions: None.

KENTUCKY
Inheritance Tax: Inheriting spouse, child or parent pays 2-10 percent; brother or sister pays 4-16 percent; all others pay 6-16 percent.
Property exempt from taxation: $50,000 for spouse; $20,000 for child; $5,000 for parent; $1,000 for brother or sister; $500 for all others.
Estate Tax: None.
Credit Estate Tax: Yes.
Special Provisions: None.

LOUISIANA
Inheritance Tax: Inheriting spouse, child or parent pays 2-3 percent; brother or sister pays 5-7 percent; all others pay 5-10 percent.
Property exempt from taxation: $10,000 for spouse, child or parent (increasing to $15,000 for the estates of persons dying in 1985 and to $20,000 for estates of persons dying in 1986); $1,000 for brother or sister; $500 for all others.
Estate Tax: None.
Credit Estate Tax: Yes.
Special Provisions: None.

MAINE
Inheritance Tax: Repealed for estates of persons dying after June 30, 1986. Until then, inheriting spouse, child or parent pays 5-10 percent; brother or sister pays 8-14 percent; all others pay 14-18 percent.
Property exempt from taxation: $50,000 for spouse; $25,000 for child or parent; $1,000 for all others.
Estate Tax: None.
Credit Estate Tax: Yes.
Special Provisions: None.

MARYLAND
Inheritance Tax: Inheriting spouse, child or parent pays 1 percent; all others pay 10 percent.
Property exempt from taxation: $150 for all persons.
Estate Tax: None.
Credit Estate Tax: Yes.
Special Provisions: None.

MASSACHUSETTS
Inheritance Tax: None.
Estate Tax: 5-6 percent.
Property exempt from taxation: Total exemption for all estates with net value of less than $60,000; all others, $30,000 exemption.
Credit Estate Tax: Yes.
Special Provisions: None.

MICHIGAN
Inheritance Tax: Inheriting spouse, child, parent, brother or sister pays 2-10 percent; all others pay 12-17 percent.
Property exempt from taxation: $65,000 for spouse plus $5,000 for each minor child who does not inherit property; $10,000 for child, parent, brother or sister; none for all others, except that Michigan charitable, religious and educational associations are entirely exempt.
Estate Tax: None.
Credit Estate Tax: Yes.
Special Provisions: In certain cases the entire amount transferred to a surviving spouse may be exempted.

MINNESOTA
Inheritance Tax: None.
Estate Tax: None.
Credit Estate Tax: Yes.
Special Provisions: None.

MISSISSIPPI
Inheritance Tax: None.
Estate Tax: 1-16 percent. Property exempt from taxation: $60,000.
Credit Estate Tax: Yes.
Special Provisions: None.

MISSOURI
Inheritance Tax: None.
Estate Tax: None.
Credit Estate Tax: Yes.
Special Provisions: None.

MONTANA
Inheritance Tax: Inheriting spouse, child or parent pays 2-8 percent; brother or sister pays 4-16 percent; all others pay 8-32 percent.
Property exempt from taxation: All for spouse or child; $7,000 for parent; $1,000 for brother or sister; none for all others.
Estate Tax: None.

Credit Estate Tax: Yes.
Special Provisions: None.

NEBRASKA
Inheritance Tax: Inheriting spouse, child, parent, brother or sister pays 1 percent; all others pay 6-18 percent.
Property exempt from taxation: $10,000 for spouse, child, parent, brother or sister; $500 for all others.
Estate Tax: None.
Credit Estate Tax: Yes.
Special Provisions: None.

NEVADA
Inheritance Tax: None.
Estate Tax: None.
Credit Estate Tax: None.
Special Provisions: None.

NEW HAMPSHIRE
Inheritance Tax: Inheriting spouse, child or parent pays no tax; all others pay 15 percent.
Property exempt from taxation: All for spouse, child or parent; none for all others.
Estate Tax: None.
Credit Estate Tax: Yes.
Special Provisions: Homestead exempt if used as a home.

NEW JERSEY
Inheritance Tax: Inheriting spouse, child or parent pays 2-16 percent; brother or sister pays 11-16 percent; all others pay 15-16 percent.
Property exempt from taxation: $15,000 for spouse, child or parent; $500 for all others if the inherited share is valued at $500 or less.
Estate Tax: None.
Credit Estate Tax: Yes.
Special Provisions: None.

NEW MEXICO
Inheritance Tax: None.
Estate Tax: None.
Credit Estate Tax: Yes.
Special Provisions: None.

NEW YORK
Inheritance Tax: None.
Estate Tax: 2-21 percent. To determine the exemptions that apply in any specific case, contact the New York Department of Taxation and Revenue.

Credit Estate Tax: Yes.
Special Provisions: None.

NORTH CAROLINA
Inheritance Tax: Inheriting spouse, child or parent pays 1-12 percent; brother or sister pays 4-16 percent; all others pay 8-17 percent.
Property exempt from taxation: $3,150 for spouse; none for all others.
Estate Tax: None.
Credit Estate Tax: Yes.
Special Provisions: If there is no surviving spouse or if the surviving spouse has not used all of the allowed credit, the remaining amount can be transferred to certain others.

NORTH DAKOTA
Inheritance Tax: None.
Estate Tax: None.
Credit Estate Tax: Yes.
Special Provisions: None.

OHIO
Inheritance Tax: None.
Estate Tax: 2-7 percent.
Property exempt from taxation: $60,000 for surviving spouse; $14,000 for each minor child; $6,000 for each adult child; $10,000 for all others.
Credit Estate Tax: Yes.
Special Provisions: None.

OKLAHOMA
Inheritance Tax: None.
Estate Tax: 0.5-15 percent.
Property exempt from taxation: All for surviving spouse; $175,000 for lineal heirs.
Credit Estate Tax: Yes.
Special Provisions: None.

OREGON
Inheritance Tax: None.
Estate Tax: 12 percent.
Property exempt from taxation: $200,000 for estates of persons dying in 1983 or 1984; $500,000 for estates of persons dying in 1985 or 1986; no tax after 1986.
Credit Estate Tax: Yes.
Special Provisions: Although the tax is called an inheritance tax, it has the effect of an estate tax because it is levied against the estate, not the heir.

Appendix II

PENNSYLVANIA
Inheritance Tax: Inheriting spouse, child or parent pays 6 percent; all others pay 15 percent
Property exempt from taxation: None.
Estate Tax: None.
Credit Estate Tax: Yes.
Special Provisions: None.

PUERTO RICO
Inheritance Tax: None.
Estate Tax: None.
Credit Estate Tax: Yes.
Special Provisions: None.

RHODE ISLAND
Inheritance Tax: None.
Estate Tax: 2-9 percent.
Property exempt from taxation: $175,000 for a surviving spouse; otherwise, $25,000.
Credit Estate Tax: Yes.
Special Provisions: None.

SOUTH CAROLINA
Inheritance Tax: None.
Estate Tax: 6-8 percent.
Property exempt from taxation: Unlimited marital deduction for surviving spouse, similar to federal taxation rules; otherwise, $120,000.
Credit Estate Tax: Yes.
Special Provisions: None.

SOUTH DAKOTA
Inheritance Tax: Inheriting spouse, child or parent pays 3-7.5 percent; brother or sister pays 10-20 percent; all others pay 15-30 percent.
Property exempt from taxation: All for spouse; $30,000 for child; $3,000 for parent; $500 for brother or sister; $200 for aunt, uncle or their descendants; $100 for all others.
Estate Tax: None.
Credit Estate Tax: Yes.
Special Provisions: None.

TENNESSEE
Inheritance Tax: Inheriting spouse, child, parent, brother or sister pays 5.5-9.5 percent; all others pay 6.5-16 percent.
Property exempt from taxation: $325,000 for spouse, child, parent, brother or sister; $10,000 for all others.
Estate Tax: None.

Credit Estate Tax: Yes.
Special Provisions: For spouse, child, parent, brother or sister, plus for certain others related by marriage, the exemptions increase each year following the schedule of federal tax exemption increases. See Chart, page 7.

TEXAS
Inheritance Tax: Inheriting spouse, child or parent pays 1-6 percent; brother or sister pays 3-10 percent; all others pay 5-20 percent.
Property exempt from taxation: Spouse, child and parent share one exemption up to $200,000 but not less than $25,000; $10,000 for brother or sister; $500 for all others.
Estate Tax: None.
Credit Estate Tax: Yes.
Special Provisions: None.

UTAH
Inheritance Tax: None.
Estate Tax: None. Repealed for estates of persons dying after January 1, 1977.
Credit Estate Tax: Yes.
Special Provisions: None.

VERMONT
Inheritance Tax: None.
Estate Tax: None.
Credit Estate Tax: Yes.
Special Provisions: None.

VIRGINIA
Inheritance Tax: None.
Estate Tax: None.
Credit Estate Tax: Yes.
Special Provisions: None.

VIRGIN ISLANDS
Inheritance Tax: Inheriting spouse, child or parent pays 5 percent; brother or sister pays 10 percent; all others pay 15 percent.
Property exempt from taxation: $50,000 for spouse, child or parent; $30,000 for brother or sister; $5,000 for all others.
Estate Tax: None.
Credit Estate Tax: Yes.
Special Provisions: None.

Appendix II

WASHINGTON
Inheritance Tax: None. Repealed for estates of persons dying after December 31, 1982.
Estate Tax: None.
Credit Estate Tax: Yes.
Special Provisions: None.

WEST VIRGINIA
Inheritance Tax: Inheriting spouse, child or parent pays 3-13 percent; brother or sister pays 4-18 percent; all others pay 10-30 percent.
Property exempt from taxation: $30,000 for spouse; $10,000 for child, parent, brother or sister; $200 for all others.
Estate Tax: None.
Credit Estate Tax: Yes.
Special Provisions: None.

WISCONSIN
Inheritance Tax: Inheriting spouse, child or parent pays 2.5-12.5 percent; brother or sister pays 5-25 percent; all others pay 7.5-30 percent.
Property exempt from taxation: All for spouse; $10,000 for child or parent; $1,000 for brother or sister; $500-1,000 for all others.
Estate Tax: None.
Credit Estate Tax: Yes.
Special Provisions: None.

WYOMING
Inheritance Tax: None. Repealed for estates of persons dying after December 31, 1982.
Estate Tax: None.
Credit Estate Tax: Yes.
Special Provisions: None.

HALT

HALT — An Organization of Americans for Legal Reform is a national nonpartisan public interest group of more than 100,000 members. It is dedicated to the principle that all people in the United States should be able to dispose of their legal affairs in a simple, affordable and equitable manner. HALT works to:

•Increase awareness that people can — and should be able to — handle their own civil legal affairs.

•Reduce the number of cases that clog our courts by eliminating unnecessary litigation and promoting alternative ways of resolving disputes.

•Simplify the civil court system and its procedures and make it accountable to the public.

To accomplish these goals, HALT publishes its *Citizens Legal Manuals* series and a variety of one-page guides to the basic principles and procedures of the legal system. These materials are all written in simple, easy-to-understand language. They include step-by-step "how to" instructions, lists of other resources and explanations of the law and citizens' rights and responsibilities.

HALT's quarterly magazine, *Americans for Legal Reform*, is the nation's top publication of legal reform news, analysis and opinion. It keeps members informed about major legal reform efforts and what they can do to help. Regular features include book reviews, a Legal Advisor column and legislative updates.

In state legislatures and the U.S. Congress, HALT supports:

•Reforming "Unauthorized Practice of Law" (UPL) by which state bar associations forbid nonlawyers to handle routine, uncontested matters.

- Public participation in open and effective procedures for disciplining judges and lawyers and settling disputes between lawyers and clients.

- Efficient and equitable no-fault systems of compensating victims for their injuries — whether from auto collisions, product or environmental hazards or medical malpractice.

- Standard do-it-yourself forms for routine, uncontested divorces, wills and other legal matters.

- Plain-language standards for all legal documents.

- Simplified probate procedures, eliminating unnecessary lawyer-involvement in probate and prohibiting probate lawyers from collecting a percentage of the estate rather than an hourly or flat fee.

- Requiring mediation, arbitration or other out-of-court methods of resolving a wide variety of disputes.

All HALT's activities are funded by member contributions. Since its founding in 1978, HALT has been instrumental in achieving reforms in several states from Maine to California, but much more needs to be done. You can help by joining HALT or enrolling a friend. Your contributions are tax deductible. For further information, write:

HALT, Inc.
1319 F Street NW, Suite 300
Washington, D.C. 20004
(202) 347-9600